HEAD to HEAD

Schiffer Kids

4880 Lower Valley Road, Atglen, PA 19310

This book would not have been possible without the help of my wife, Annika, and my parents, Joanne and Bruno.

Baptist Cornabas

ISBN: 978-0-7643-6226-2
Printed in China

Published by Schiffer Kids
An imprint of Schiffer Publishing, Ltd.
4880 Lower Valley Road
Atglen, PA 19310
Phone: (610) 593-1777; Fax: (610) 593-2002
E-mail: Info@schifferbooks.com
Web: www.schifferbooks.com

For our complete selection of fine books on this and related subjects, please visit our website at www.schifferbooks.com. You may also write for a free catalog.

Schiffer Publishing's titles are available at special discounts for bulk purchases for sales promotions or premiums. Special editions, including personalized covers, corporate imprints, and excerpts, can be created in large quantities for special needs. For more information, contact the publisher.

FSC
www.fsc.org
MIX
Paper from
responsible sources
FSC® C020560

HEAD to HEAD

18 LINKED PORTRAITS OF PEOPLE
WHO CHANGED THE WORLD

WRITTEN BY BAPTIST CORNABAS
ILLUSTRATED BY ANTOINE CORBINEAU

CONTENTS

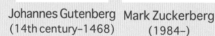

INTRODUCTION

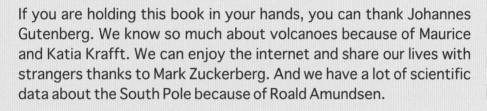

If you are holding this book in your hands, you can thank Johannes Gutenberg. We know so much about volcanoes because of Maurice and Katia Krafft. We can enjoy the internet and share our lives with strangers thanks to Mark Zuckerberg. And we have a lot of scientific data about the South Pole because of Roald Amundsen.

The world is full of people—some ordinary, some extraordinary—who rethink and revolutionize our daily lives. They perform amazing work, fight for rights and freedom, and seek to discover what is hidden or unknown. But giving you a list of these change-makers is not the point of this book. Instead, we will compare eighteen people—nine pairs— who have left their mark during their lifetime. They have not always been perfect, but they have tried to make our world a better place.

Did you know that Mother Teresa and Angelina Jolie have something in common? Can you guess what connects Leonardo da Vinci and Steve Jobs? Or Gandhi and Rosa Parks? These people did not live at the same time and never met each other, yet there is one thing that unites them.

Will you understand what links these fascinating pairs just by looking at their portraits? Probably not. But just open the folded pages. Inside, you will find biographies of each person and an explanation that helps you understand the common point between the two people.

After you read about each pair, turn the page and you'll see a timeline that places them within the context of history. At the end of the book is a map that shows where each of these people was born. Maybe some have lived near you.

So now let's go head to head!

THEY WERE
AHEAD

Leonardo da Vinci invented a helicopter that could not fly, a diving suit that would have drowned its wearer, a parachute that was too heavy, a car that did not run, and a tank that could not move without horses. When Steve Jobs introduced the iPhone to the public in January 2007, its many bugs frustrated users. It was impossible to play an entire video or run certain applications without causing the phone to restart.

We should not judge these setbacks too harshly, though. Why? Because they did lead to success. Most of the inventions that Leonardo dreamed up now exist, and Steve's iPhones have been sold to nearly two billion people!

TODAY, MOST OF LEONARDO DA VINCI'S INVENTIONS EXIST, AND MORE THAN TWO BILLION IPHONES HAVE BEEN SOLD THROUGHOUT THE WORLD.

Back in the sixteenth century, Leonardo's designs for flying machines were unlike anything anyone had ever seen. They looked radical but were based on the simple idea that the air is thick and objects can glide on it, which is just what today's airplanes do. Leonardo simply lacked the modern materials and technology to make his creations work. As proof, in 2008, a Swiss man named Olivier Vietti-Teppa jumped from a helicopter while wearing Leonardo's parachute design, which was made of lightweight and flexible material. His jump was a success!

Not many of Leonardo's contemporaries were aware of his wide-ranging ideas and interests. These were revealed only later, when his notebooks were studied. The books' 13,000 pages are filled with writing and drawings of people, the natural world, and his many inventions.

Leonardo DA VINCI

(1452–1519)

Leonardo DA VINCI

Painter, inventor, engineer, scientist, sculptor, architect, botanist, musician, poet, humanist, and philosopher—yes, it is possible for one person to do all of these jobs! But to do so, you would have to be Leonardo da Vinci.

Leonardo di ser Piero da Vinci was born on April 15, 1452, in Vinci, a small town in Tuscany, Italy. When translated, his name means Leonardo, son of Master Piero (his father's first name) of Vinci. You might be wondering why he was named after his hometown. At that time, family names were often used by only the richest people. For others, it was common to give the name of the place where they lived.

In 1466, when Leonardo was fourteen years old, his family moved to the city of Florence. That is when he started drawing. He turned out to be quite talented, and at age seventeen he joined the studio of an artist named Andrea del Verrocchio. It was from Verrocchio that Leonardo learned about painting, drawing, architecture, and sculpture.

In 1478, Leonardo left Verrocchio's studio and became an independent painter. In the years that followed, he was employed in various cities. In Milan, he worked as an engineer, painter, and organizer of royal celebrations. In Venice, he was hired as an architect and military engineer, tasked with protecting the city from a naval attack by outside forces.

In 1503, when Leonardo was fifty-one years old, he returned to Florence, where he was hired as an engineer and urban planner. This is where he began his most famous painting, known as the *Mona Lisa*. Although this portrait is celebrated all over the world, no one seems to know exactly who the woman in the painting is.

In 1516, the French king Francis I invited Leonardo to settle in France. He gave him a grand manor house near Amboise to live and work in. Leonardo died at Le Clos Lucé in 1519, at the age of sixty-seven.

Steve JOBS

If you have a smartphone in your backpack, it is partly thanks to Steve Jobs, who made the technology popular.

Steve was born on February 24, 1955, in San Francisco to a Syrian-born father and a Swiss-born American mother. He was adopted by Paul and Clara Jobs.

As a boy, Steve was passionate about electronics. At age thirteen, he worked for the technology company Hewlett-Packard. HP was developing one of the first personal computers, the 9100A, which looked like a big calculator. Steve's passion was shared by his classmate Steve Wozniak, with whom he would go on to create Apple.

After graduating from high school in 1972, Steve started college, but he quickly grew bored. Two years later, he returned to his parents' home and got a job at Atari. With games like Pong and Asteroids, Atari was considered the founder of the video game industry.

In 1976, the Apple adventure began in the Jobs family's garage. Steve and his friend Steve Wozniak developed the Apple I, one of the first personal microcomputers. Today's computers are much more powerful, but at the time, the Apple I was revolutionary.

The company's success came with its second computer, the Apple II. Due to a disagreement, Steve Jobs left Apple in 1985. He founded a new company, NeXT, which manufactured computers and software.

In 1986, Steve bought the computer graphics division of Lucasfilm. It was renamed Pixar and became known for such computer-animated films as *Toy Story* and *Coco*. Steve had thought he was done with Apple after resigning from his job back in 1985. But in 1997, Apple decided to buy NeXT, and Steve became its president.

Under Steve's direction, Apple released several revolutionary products: the iMac in 1998, the iPod and iTunes in 2001, and the iPad in 2010. But the device that truly changed our lives and the way we communicate was the iPhone. It was presented to the public for the first time in 2007.

In 2003, Steve Jobs learned that he had cancer. He fought the disease for many years and had surgery to remove the tumor, but the cancer returned. He died on October 5, 2011, at his home in Palo Alto, California. He was fifty-six years old.

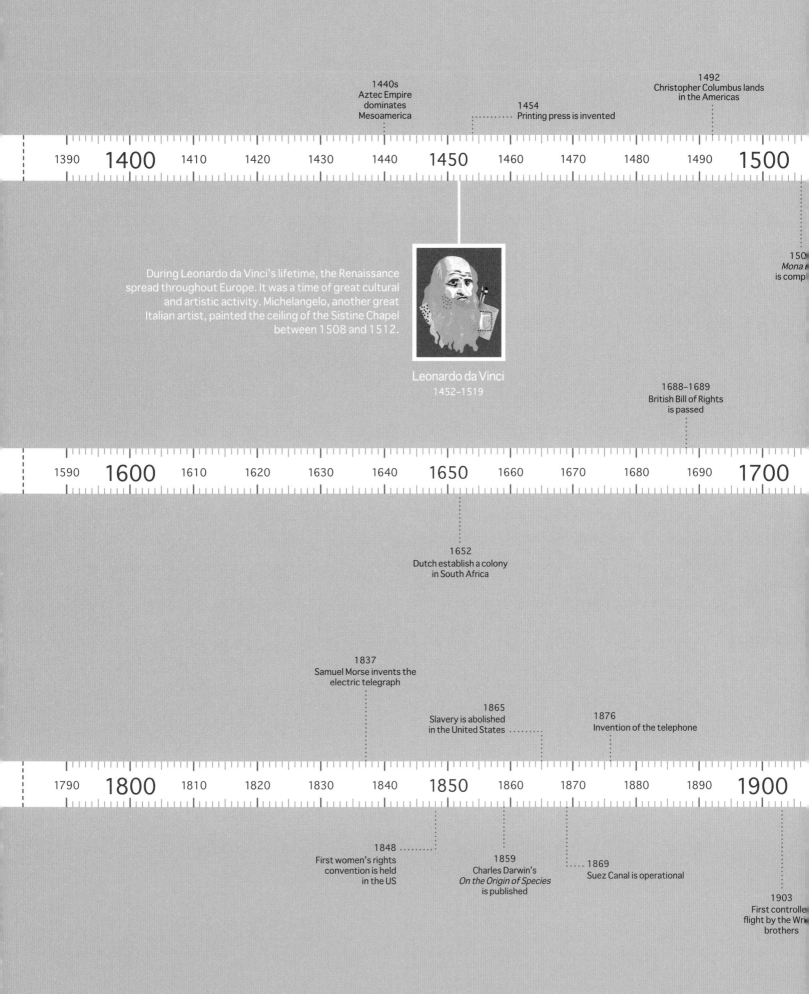

1440s
Aztec Empire
dominates
Mesoamerica

1454
Printing press is invented

1492
Christopher Columbus lands
in the Americas

1390 **1400** 1410 1420 1430 1440 **1450** 1460 1470 1480 1490 **1500**

150
Mona l
is comp

During Leonardo da Vinci's lifetime, the Renaissance
spread throughout Europe. It was a time of great cultural
and artistic activity. Michelangelo, another great
Italian artist, painted the ceiling of the Sistine Chapel
between 1508 and 1512.

Leonardo da Vinci
1452–1519

1688–1689
British Bill of Rights
is passed

1590 **1600** 1610 1620 1630 1640 **1650** 1660 1670 1680 1690 **1700**

1652
Dutch establish a colony
in South Africa

1837
Samuel Morse invents the
electric telegraph

1865
Slavery is abolished
in the United States

1876
Invention of the telephone

1790 **1800** 1810 1820 1830 1840 **1850** 1860 1870 1880 1890 **1900**

1848
First women's rights
convention is held
in the US

1859
Charles Darwin's
On the Origin of Species
is published

1869
Suez Canal is operational

1903
First controlle
flight by the Wri
brothers

VISIONARIES OF THEIR TIME

In 2007, the smartphone was not common like it is today. Steve Jobs launched his device after other manufacturers had failed with their own. In the early 2000s, the stars of the mobile phones were the Nokia 3210 and 3310, which, together, sold nearly 300 million devices. These phones had tiny screens, compared to today's smartphones, but they were appreciated for their shock resistance and strong battery, which could last several weeks. In 2007, smartphones such as the Nokia N95, the Blackberry 8300 Curve, and the Palm Centro already existed. These models were essential more ten years ago but are mostly forgotten today.

Although the smartphone was available before Apple, Steve's iPhone put the internet right in everyone's pocket. It has also allowed for the creation of a huge number of applications that allow us to tweet, send messages, play games, watch videos, and even make phone calls from time to time. ◼

LEONARDO DA VINCI AND STEVE JOBS:
EACH IMAGINED MACHINES THAT CHANGED
THE WORLD.

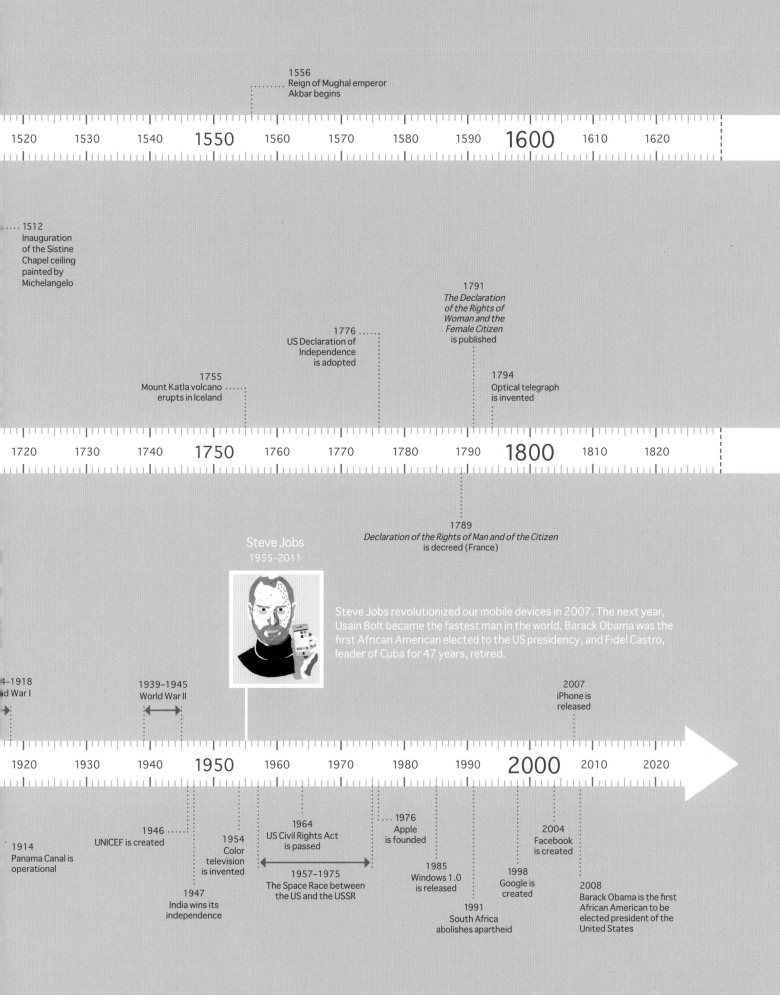

1556
Reign of Mughal emperor
Akbar begins

1520　1530　1540　**1550**　1560　1570　1580　1590　**1600**　1610　1620

1512
Inauguration
of the Sistine
Chapel ceiling
painted by
Michelangelo

1791
*The Declaration
of the Rights of
Woman and the
Female Citizen*
is published

1776
US Declaration of
Independence
is adopted

1794
Optical telegraph
is invented

1755
Mount Katla volcano
erupts in Iceland

1720　1730　1740　**1750**　1760　1770　1780　1790　**1800**　1810　1820

1789
Declaration of the Rights of Man and of the Citizen
is decreed (France)

Steve Jobs
1955-2011

Steve Jobs revolutionized our mobile devices in 2007. The next year,
Usain Bolt became the fastest man in the world, Barack Obama was the
first African American elected to the US presidency, and Fidel Castro,
leader of Cuba for 47 years, retired.

4-1918
d War I

1939-1945
World War II

2007
iPhone is
released

1920　1930　1940　**1950**　1960　1970　1980　1990　**2000**　2010　2020

1946
UNICEF is created

1964
US Civil Rights Act
is passed

1976
Apple
is founded

2004
Facebook
is created

1914
Panama Canal is
operational

1954
Color
television
is invented

1985
Windows 1.0
is released

1998
Google is
created

2008
Barack Obama is the first
African American to be
elected president of the
United States

1957-1975
The Space Race between
the US and the USSR

1947
India wins its
independence

1991
South Africa
abolishes apartheid

THEY

One resisted the Vichy regime; the other resisted apartheid. Both Jean Moulin and Nelson Mandela stood firm in the face of danger.

In 1910, the Union of South Africa was created as a self-governing nation within the British Empire. Soon after, the first racist laws were passed.

Black people were excluded from politics and all important occupations; they were also deprived of the right to vote and the freedom of movement. It was in this context that the African National Congress, or ANC, was founded to defend the rights of all Africans.

NELSON MANDELA REFUSED TO OBEY THE RACIST LAWS OF APARTHEID.

Nelson Mandela joined the party in 1943 and became its vice president in 1952. With the ANC, he led campaigns of civil disobedience by publicly refusing to submit to apartheid laws. Nelson was arrested, sentenced to nine months in prison, and banned from all meetings.

In 1955, Nelson participated in the drafting of the Charter of Freedom, a text that called for equality among all South Africans. After a massacre by the police during a peaceful demonstration, Nelson decided to fight back using weapons. He coordinated acts of sabotage against the government. Between 1961 and 1963, there were 190 ANC attacks, resulting in many countries considering the party a terrorist organization. Nelson was arrested on August 5, 1962, and kept in prison for twenty-seven years. It was only after his release in 1990 that he was able to abolish apartheid laws peacefully.

Jean MOULIN

(1899–1943)

Jean
MOULIN

Jean Moulin is a symbol of the French people's resistance to Nazi occupation during the Second World War. He was born on June 20, 1899, in the southern French town of Béziers. Jean's childhood was peaceful, and he had a passion for drawing. In fact, his drawings were so good that he was able to sell some to local newspapers. In 1917, during the First World War, seventeen-year-old Jean enrolled in the Faculty of Law of Montpellier and joined the cabinet of the prefect of the Hérault department.

The war caught up with Jean when he turned eighteen. He was mobilized and then stationed in the Vosges, in eastern France. He narrowly missed being sent to the battlefront. His regiment was preparing to go, but the armistice that ended the war was signed in November 1918.

Jean took up his life where he had left it. He returned to the prefecture and continued his studies, earning his law license in 1921. In 1925, he became the youngest sub-prefect in France and held a series of positions in different towns.

In 1939, the Second World War began. Jean wanted to fight in the battle, but the minister told him to remain prefect. Nazi troops invaded France in May 1940, and on June 17 Jean was arrested and then tortured. The pro-German Vichy government forced Jean to resign, and in October 1941, he moved to London, where he wanted to join the Resistance. He met with the French general Charles de Gaulle, who gave Jean a special task: coordinate all the Resistance movements under his leadership. Jean returned to France in 1942 to do this job.

Jean succeeded in his mission in 1943 when he founded the National Council of the Resistance. This organization united the varied resistance movements and allowed France to stand alongside the winners of the war, despite the German invasion. While the council was meeting on June 21, 1943, Nazi troops came to arrest Jean. During his interrogation, the Gestapo tortured him. He died while being transported to Germany in the summer of 1943. He had revealed no information to the enemy.

Nelson MANDELA

(1918–2013)

1440s
Aztec Empire dominates Mesoamerica

1454
Printing press is invented

1492
Christopher Columbus lands in the Americas

| | 1390 | 1400 | 1410 | 1420 | 1430 | 1440 | 1450 | 1460 | 1470 | 1480 | 1490 | 1500 |

Leonardo da Vinci

15
Mona
is com

1652
Dutch establish a colony in South Africa

1688–1689
British Bill of Rights is passed

| | 1590 | 1600 | 1610 | 1620 | 1630 | 1640 | 1650 | 1660 | 1670 | 1680 | 1690 | 1700 |

Jean Moulin
1899–1943

Jean Moulin lived in troubled times. In 1921, Ireland divided into two states; in 1928, Stalin asserted his power over the USSR, and Yugoslavia became a dictatorship; in 1929, the world sank into an economic crisis that encouraged the rise of extremism in Europe. The major event during Jean Moulin's life was the Second World War, the deadliest conflict in history.

1837
Samuel Morse invents the electric telegraph

1865
Slavery is abolished in the United States

1876
Invention of the telephone

1903
First cont
flight by t
Wright br

| | 1790 | 1800 | 1810 | 1820 | 1830 | 1840 | 1850 | 1860 | 1870 | 1880 | 1890 | 1900 |

1848
First women's rights convention is held in the US

1859
Charles Darwin's On the Origin of Species is published

1869
Suez Canal is operational

1914
Panama Canal is operational

RESISTED

Jean Moulin began his resistance at the same time for different reasons. It was while he was serving as prefect in central France that Nazi troops attacked Western Europe, on May 10, 1940. They advanced quickly because of a tactic unknown until then: the Blitzkrieg, or "lightning war," which made it possible to break through the French lines. Paris was captured on June 14, and Jean's town of Chartres fell the next day.

On June 17, German officers ordered Jean, as a government official, to sign a racist text. He refused. The Nazis then arrested him and put him in prison. After he was released from jail, he joined General Charles de Gaulle in London. The general asked Jean to return to France to unite the different resistance movements under his leadership.

In the spring of 1943, Jean succeeded in creating the National Council of Resistance. The CNR directed and coordinated the various resistance movements to make them more effective. Unlike Nelson, who lived to see results of his efforts, Jean was unable to witness the liberation of France. He was killed by the Nazis in 1943, two years before the end of the war. ■

JEAN MOULIN AND NELSON MANDELA STOOD FIRM IN THE FACE OF ADVERSITY.

Nelson MANDELA

Nelson Mandela's real first name was Rolihlahla, which means "troublemaker" in his native Xhosa language. He was born on July 18, 1918, in Mvezo, South Africa, and had thirteen brothers and sisters. Rolihlahla was the first member of his family to attend an elementary school. His teacher gave him an English name, Nelson, which was a common custom at the time. South Africa had been a British colony between 1806 and 1910. Although the region acquired some autonomy as a dominion, it remained in the British Empire. At an early age, Nelson became aware of the oppression of Africans, who had fewer and fewer rights under colonial white rule.

In 1939, Nelson entered the University of Fort Hare to study law. Because of his activism, he was suspended in his second year. He then moved to Johannesburg to escape an arranged marriage. He continued studying law, worked in a law firm, and, in 1943, joined the African National Congress. This South African political party sought to defend the interests of the black majority against the white minority. He married in 1944.

In 1948, the fate of Nelson and the country of South Africa changed forever. That year, the elections were won by the National Party, which enacted racist laws to preserve white supremacy. Under this policy, which became known as apartheid, white and black people were officially separated. Nelson fought against these unfair laws. He was arrested in 1962 and sentenced to prison and hard labor. He became known worldwide as a symbol of the struggle for racial equality.

On February 2, 1990, after spending twenty-seven years, six months, and six days in prison, Nelson was released. On that day, he delivered a speech in favor of peace and reconciliation with the country's white minority. Gradually, apartheid laws were abolished because of his actions and the cooperation of South Africa's president, F. W. de Klerk. Both men received the Nobel Peace Prize in 1993.

On April 27, 1994, the first universal elections were held in South Africa, and Nelson Mandela became its first black president. In 1999, he retired from politics and devoted more time to his family. He died on December 5, 2013, at the age of ninety-five.

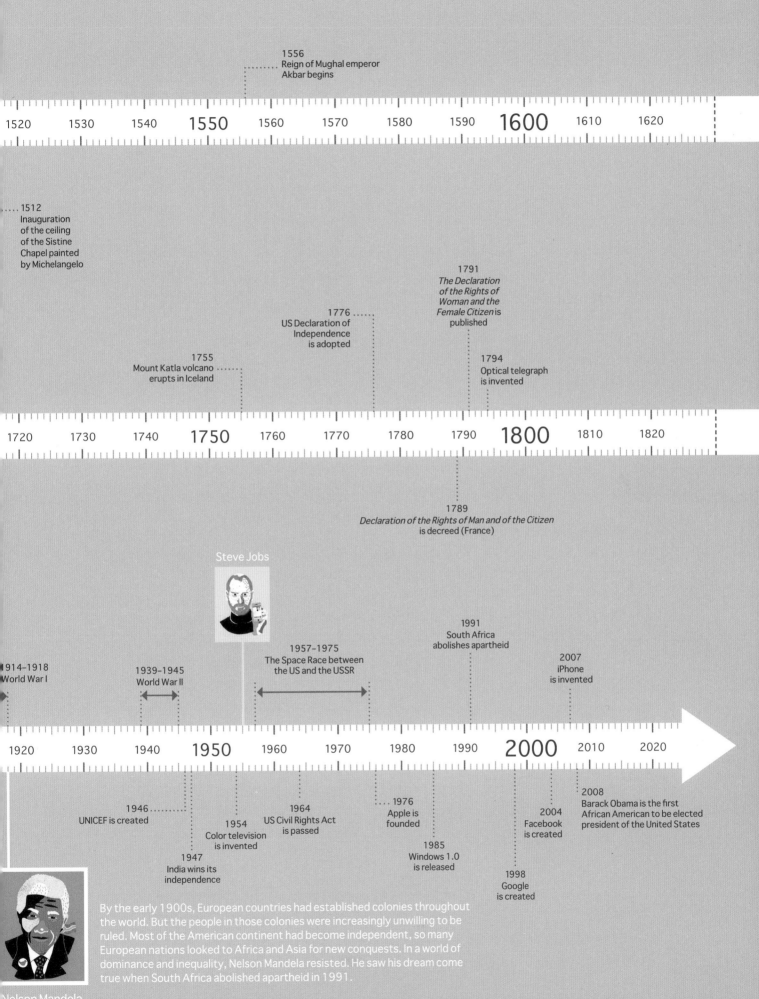

1556
Reign of Mughal emperor
Akbar begins

1520 | 1530 | 1540 | **1550** | 1560 | 1570 | 1580 | 1590 | **1600** | 1610 | 1620

1512
Inauguration
of the ceiling
of the Sistine
Chapel painted
by Michelangelo

1791
*The Declaration
of the Rights of
Woman and the
Female Citizen* is
published

1776
US Declaration of
Independence
is adopted

1755
Mount Katla volcano
erupts in Iceland

1794
Optical telegraph
is invented

1720 | 1730 | 1740 | **1750** | 1760 | 1770 | 1780 | 1790 | **1800** | 1810 | 1820

1789
Declaration of the Rights of Man and of the Citizen
is decreed (France)

Steve Jobs

1991
South Africa
abolishes apartheid

2007
iPhone
is invented

1957–1975
The Space Race between
the US and the USSR

1939–1945
World War II

1914–1918
World War I

1920 | 1930 | 1940 | **1950** | 1960 | 1970 | 1980 | 1990 | **2000** | 2010 | 2020

1946
UNICEF is created

1954
Color television
is invented

1964
US Civil Rights Act
is passed

1976
Apple is
founded

2004
Facebook
is created

2008
Barack Obama is the first
African American to be elected
president of the United States

1947
India wins its
independence

1985
Windows 1.0
is released

1998
Google
is created

By the early 1900s, European countries had established colonies throughout
the world. But the people in those colonies were increasingly unwilling to be
ruled. Most of the American continent had become independent, so many
European nations looked to Africa and Asia for new conquests. In a world of
dominance and inequality, Nelson Mandela resisted. He saw his dream come
true when South Africa abolished apartheid in 1991.

Nelson Mandela
1918–2013

THEY FOUGHT WITHOUT

After slavery was abolished in the United States in the 1800s, laws were passed to maintain a strict separation of black and white people. They were prohibited from marrying each other and sitting together on public transportation. Rosa grew up during racial segregation. She decided to fight against this discrimination in a nonviolent way.

Rosa's activism began in 1943, when she became a member of NAACP, the National Association for the Advancement of Colored People. She was angry that so few African Americans could register to vote. Black men had been granted the right to vote in 1870, and black women had gained suffrage in 1920. But, in reality, most were unable to exercise this right because of rules and policies that prevented them from registering.

In 1945, after three attempts, Rosa finally succeeded in registering to vote. She was not the only person, nor the first, to fight for the rights of black people. It was her act of civil disobedience a decade later that brought about real change. After she was arrested for refusing to give up her seat on a bus in 1955, the local NAACP president bailed her out of prison. He then used his connections to rally the black community to boycott the bus company. The protest was led by a local pastor named Martin Luther King Jr., who became a leader in the nonviolent struggle for the civil rights of African Americans. Another model for Martin Luther King was Gandhi.

> ROSA PARKS CHOSE TO FIGHT AGAINST DISCRIMINATION IN A NONVIOLENT WAY.

Gandhi began his nonviolent struggle while living in South Africa between 1893 and 1915. He entered politics and founded the Natal Indian Congress to defend the rights of the Indian community. This party inspired Nelson Mandela's African National Congress.

GANDHI

Mohandas Karamchand Gandhi was born on October 2, 1869, in Porbandar, India, then a part of the British Empire. The word *Gandhi* means "grocer," and it comes from the caste (social class) to which his family belonged. Gandhi was raised as a Hindu, but he also learned about other religions, such as Jainism. The Jain religion promotes non-violence and respect for all human and animal life.

When Gandhi was thirteen years old, he married Kasturbai, who was fourteen. Kasturbai's parents had chosen Gandhi for their daughter, a practice known as an arranged marriage. The couple got along well, and Kasturbai was loyal to her husband until the end of her life.

In 1888, when Gandhi was eighteen, he went alone to England to study law. He finished in 1891 and returned to India, but he was not successful as a lawyer. In 1893, he moved with his family to South Africa. A large Indian community lived there, and he became an interpreter. While there, he was confronted with racism directed at black people and Indians.

Experiencing this discrimination as an immigrant set Gandhi on his path to activism. For the next twenty years, he led a struggle of non-cooperation and nonviolent resistance against the South African authorities. He was protesting the inequalities that favored white people over the black and Indian communities.

In 1915, Gandhi returned to India. After World War I ended in 1918, he pleaded for the independence of his homeland from British control. As he had in South Africa, Gandhi chose nonviolent resistance, organizing boycotts and acts of civil disobedience. Thousands of Indians joined him in the fight. He was arrested several times and spent a total of six years in prison.

On August 15, 1947, after decades of struggle with the people of India, the British finally granted the country its independence. But it did not go as planned. India was divided between Muslims and Hindus, which led to the formation of Pakistan and the current boundaries of India.

This separation caused the death of millions of people when populations were displaced. Gandhi tried to intervene between Muslims and Hindus to avoid bloodshed. He was killed by a Hindu fanatic on January 30, 1948.

GANDHI

(1869–1948)

Rosa **PARKS**

2857

(1913–2005)

Rosa
PARKS

2857

Rosa Louise McCauley was born on February 4, 1913, in Alabama. At age eleven, she began attending a school for black children. At the time, there were laws segregating whites and blacks, who were disadvantaged and subjected to racism every day. For example, Rosa had to walk to school because the school bus was reserved for white children.

Beginning in 1930, Rosa worked as a seamstress. In 1932, at age nineteen, she married Raymond Parks, a civil rights activist. Raymond was fighting to ensure that blacks and whites had the same rights as citizens of the United States. Like Raymond, Rosa became active in the American civil rights movement. In 1943, she joined the National Association for the Advancement of Colored People (NAACP).

In 1955, Rosa entered history as a hero. At that time in the city of Montgomery, Alabama, the first rows of buses were reserved for white people; black people had to sit in the seats at the back. One day, Rosa was sitting in the black seats on a crowded bus. A white man got on, and the driver told Rosa to give up her seat for him. This was too much! She refused to move. It was not the first time Rosa had resisted unfair treatment, but this time she was arrested and fined.

To support her, many black leaders, including Martin Luther King Jr., a local pastor who campaigned nonviolently for black civil rights, organized a bus boycott in Montgomery. For 381 days, thousands of people refused to ride the bus.

On November 13, 1956, the Supreme Court declared that segregation—the separation of blacks and whites—on municipal buses did not respect the US Constitution. As a result of her act and its outcome, Rosa was a symbol of the fight against racial segregation and for civil rights in the United States.

In 1964, nine years after the incident on the bus, Congress passed the Civil Rights Act, which outlawed all forms of discrimination. Legal segregation in the United States was officially ended. But Rosa continued to work for justice, calling attention to inequalities in access to housing for black people.

After the bus boycott, Rosa and her family moved to Michigan to escape death threats. She died in Detroit on October 24, 2005. Thousands of people attended her funeral, and all the flags in the country were lowered to half-mast. Even the Montgomery bus company paid her a final tribute by covering the front seats of its buses with Rosa's photo.

VIOLENCE

Like Rosa's act of defiance, Gandhi's actions against discriminatory laws were carried out nonviolently—through demonstrations, petitions, and boycotts. Later, he chose the same methods to fight against injustices in his homeland, but in India he was fighting for independence from British rule.

THE PEACEFUL ACTS OF GANDHI AND ROSA PARKS SERVED AS A MODEL FOR MARTIN LUTHER KING JR.

Gandhi developed a policy called *satyagraha*, a form of nonviolent resistance and civil disobedience. He refused to obey unjust laws, putting pressure on the authorities to annul these rules. He joined the Indian National Congress political party and became one of its main leaders. The party followed his principles of nonviolence and non-cooperation.

In 1918, Gandhi organized a boycott against the British policy of forcing Indian farmers to cultivate indigo (for dyeing clothes). The farmers could not grow the food they needed to survive, causing famine and poverty. The British authorities relented, but Gandhi's struggle was far from over. In 1930, he rose up to protest the British monopoly on salt, which prevented Indians from extracting salt from their own country. Gandhi organized a peaceful march—nearly 250 miles long—across the country and to the sea. Thousands of Indians joined him, and, together, they collected salt. This way of defying injustice peacefully has inspired many struggles and protests worldwide. ■

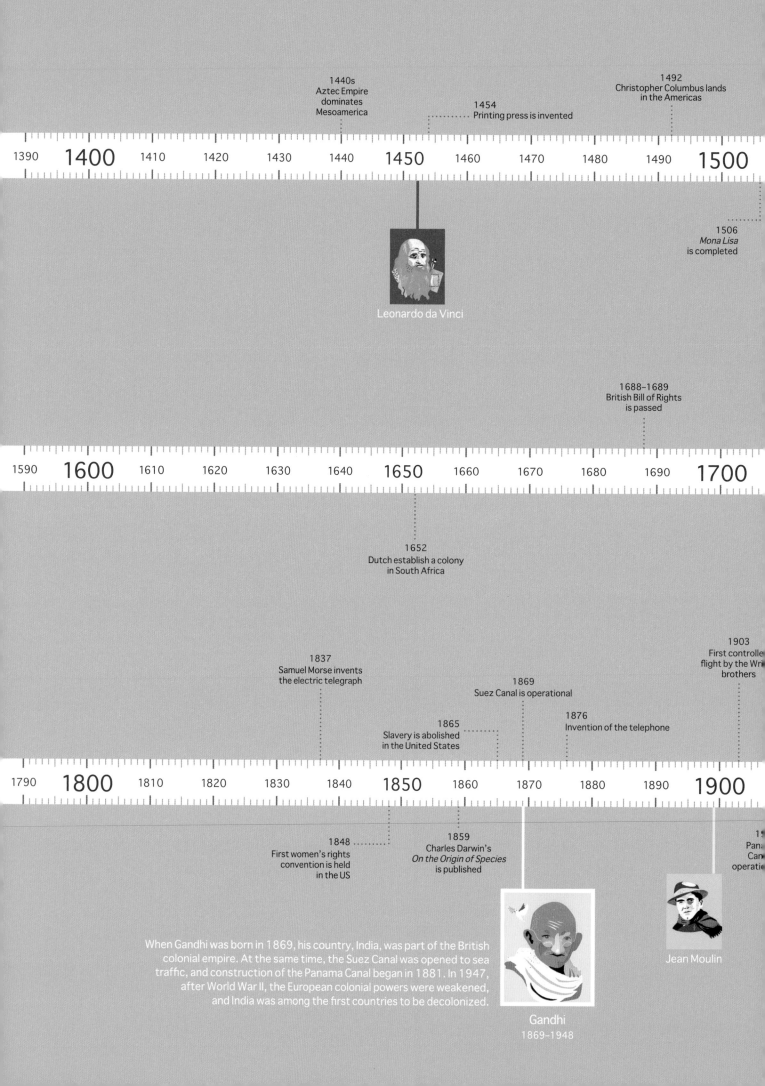

1440s
Aztec Empire
dominates
Mesoamerica

1454
Printing press is invented

1492
Christopher Columbus lands
in the Americas

1390 **1400** 1410 1420 1430 1440 **1450** 1460 1470 1480 1490 **1500**

1506
Mona Lisa
is completed

Leonardo da Vinci

1688–1689
British Bill of Rights
is passed

1590 **1600** 1610 1620 1630 1640 **1650** 1660 1670 1680 1690 **1700**

1652
Dutch establish a colony
in South Africa

1903
First controlle
flight by the Wri
brothers

1837
Samuel Morse invents
the electric telegraph

1869
Suez Canal is operational

1865
Slavery is abolished
in the United States

1876
Invention of the telephone

1790 **1800** 1810 1820 1830 1840 **1850** 1860 1870 1880 1890 **1900**

1848
First women's rights
convention is held
in the US

1859
Charles Darwin's
On the Origin of Species
is published

1
Pana
Ca
operatio

When Gandhi was born in 1869, his country, India, was part of the British
colonial empire. At the same time, the Suez Canal was opened to sea
traffic, and construction of the Panama Canal began in 1881. In 1947,
after World War II, the European colonial powers were weakened,
and India was among the first countries to be decolonized.

Jean Moulin

Gandhi
1869–1948

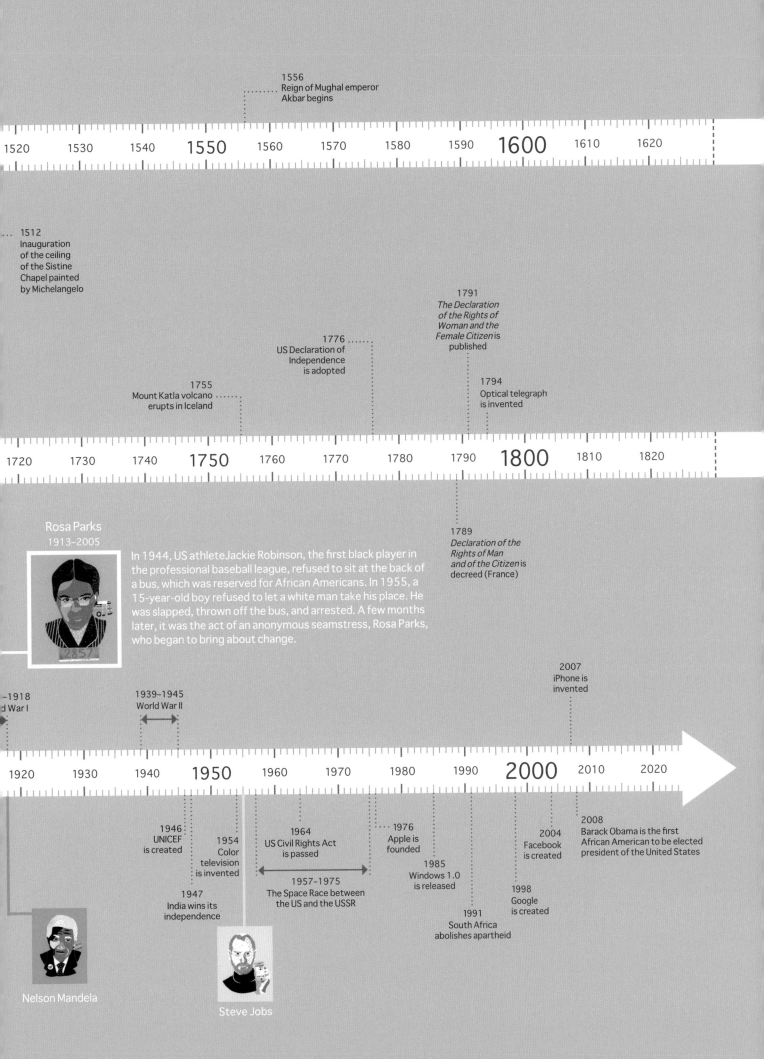

1556
Reign of Mughal emperor
Akbar begins

1520 | 1530 | 1540 | **1550** | 1560 | 1570 | 1580 | 1590 | **1600** | 1610 | 1620

1512
Inauguration
of the ceiling
of the Sistine
Chapel painted
by Michelangelo

1791
*The Declaration
of the Rights of
Woman and the
Female Citizen* is
published

1776
US Declaration of
Independence
is adopted

1755
Mount Katla volcano
erupts in Iceland

1794
Optical telegraph
is invented

1720 | 1730 | 1740 | **1750** | 1760 | 1770 | 1780 | 1790 | **1800** | 1810 | 1820

Rosa Parks
1913–2005

In 1944, US athlete Jackie Robinson, the first black player in
the professional baseball league, refused to sit at the back of
a bus, which was reserved for African Americans. In 1955, a
15-year-old boy refused to let a white man take his place. He
was slapped, thrown off the bus, and arrested. A few months
later, it was the act of an anonymous seamstress, Rosa Parks,
who began to bring about change.

1789
*Declaration of the
Rights of Man
and of the Citizen* is
decreed (France)

2007
iPhone is
invented

–1918
d War I

1939–1945
World War II

1920 | 1930 | 1940 | **1950** | 1960 | 1970 | 1980 | 1990 | **2000** | 2010 | 2020

1946
UNICEF
is created

1954
Color
television
is invented

1964
US Civil Rights Act
is passed

1976
Apple is
founded

2004
Facebook
is created

2008
Barack Obama is the first
African American to be elected
president of the United States

1985
Windows 1.0
is released

1998
Google
is created

1947
India wins its
independence

1957–1975
The Space Race between
the US and the USSR

1991
South Africa
abolishes apartheid

Nelson Mandela

Steve Jobs

THEY HELPED THE MOST

Angelina Jolie, one of Hollywood's highest-paid actresses, and Mother Teresa, who dedicated her life to helping those in need, have one thing in common: each, in her own way, came to the aid of the world's poorest people.

Teresa had always wanted to dedicate her life to the most poverty-stricken communities. In 1950, with some of her former students, she founded the Order of the Missionaries of Charity in India. She noticed that the hospitals in Kolkata could not care for all the sick and dying people. She decided to help them by founding a home where they could die in dignity. Teresa believed that their suffering was a gift from God. As a result, the patients in her centers rarely received painkillers, a practice that not everyone agrees with.

At that time, there were few orphanages in India, and many children were abandoned because their families could not afford to support them. Teresa, who believed that a woman should never have an abortion, founded the Children's Home of the Immaculate Heart in 1955 to take in orphans and other homeless youths.

MOTHER TERESA AND ANGELINA JOLIE ARE HUMANITARIANS, PEOPLE WHO HELP IMPROVE THE LIVES OF THOSE IN NEED.

Mother
TERESA

Mother Teresa was born Anjezë Gonxhe Bojaxhiu on August 26, 1910, in Üsküb, in the Ottoman Empire. Today this city is called Skopje, and it is the capital of Macedonia. Teresa's parents raised her in the Roman Catholic faith. The family often helped the poor by sharing their meals with them.

In September 1928, when Teresa was eighteen years old, she left for Ireland. She had been thinking about dedicating her life to God and began her religious training there. Two months later, Teresa moved to India to begin her novitiate, a time of deep study before entering religious life. On May 25, 1931, she took her vows and chose her religious name, Sister Mary Teresa, in honor of Thérèse of Lisieux, a French Catholic nun and saint whom she admired.

From 1931 to 1937, Teresa worked as a teacher in Calcutta (now Kolkata), India. She had classes of 300 students, who called her "Ma," which means "Mother." That led to the name by which she is known today: Mother Teresa.

In 1948, Teresa decided to leave the convent to "help the poor by living with them." From then on, she wore the white and blue-trimmed garment that she is often seen wearing in photos. She gave classes to children in the slums, cared for the poor and dying, prayed, and begged.

In 1949, a former student joined Teresa, and soon more than ten girls followed her. On October 7, 1950, Teresa founded the Order of the Missionaries of Charity. One of the order's vows is to dedicate oneself to serving the poorest of the poor and to expect nothing in return.

Mother Teresa received the Nobel Peace Prize on October 17, 1979. The Missionaries of Charity has spread across the world and now has more than 5,000 nuns. Mother Teresa died of a stomach tumor on September 5, 1997, at age eighty-seven. She was canonized (made a saint) in 2016.

Mother TERESA

(1910–1997)

Angelina JOLIE

(1975–)

Angelina JOLIE

Angelina Jolie was born in California in 1975 and grew up in a show-business family. She is the daughter of actors Jon Voight and Marcheline Bertrand. Her parents divorced when she was two years old, and Angelina was raised by her mother.

At the age of eleven, Angelina decided to become an actress. She attended the Lee Strasberg Theatre Institute of New York, a prestigious acting school. Her childhood was not the happiest: she was often teased at school because of her thinness, her clothes, or her braces.

In 1993, Angelina began her acting career with the film *Glass Shadow* after she graduated from high school. Two years later, she earned her first lead role in the film *Hackers*. Since then, she has continually made films: in the past twenty-five years, she has appeared in more than fifty movies, such as *Maleficent* and *Mr. & Mrs. Smith*.

It was her starring role in the 2001 action film *Lara Croft: Tomb Raider* that made Angelina an international star.

Filming took place in Cambodia, and the experience had a strong influence on her. She saw the effects of the war on the Cambodian people, and it drew her attention to humanitarian causes around the world.

That same year, Angelina became an ambassador for the UN's High Commissioner for Refugees (UNHCR). This humanitarian organization aims to protect people who have fled their country, and it works to find a lasting solution to their difficulties. In 2017, the UNHCR estimated that there were more than 22 million refugees worldwide.

Angelina is the mother of six children. She adopted a Cambodian boy in 2002 and an Ethiopian girl in 2005. Angelina has been married three times, including to actor Brad Pitt, with whom she had a son in 2006 and twins in 2008. In 2007, the couple adopted a Vietnamese boy who had been abandoned at birth.

POVERTY-STRICKEN

In 1963, Teresa tried in vain to oppose the destruction of a hospital for lepers. Her plea failed, but with her congregation, she helped the sick patients. Since 1965, the Missionaries of Charity has spread across the globe.

Angelina travels that same globe to help the most disadvantaged communities. She visits refugee camps in Sierra Leone, Tanzania, Thailand, Ecuador, Kenya, Pakistan, Iraq, Syria, and Namibia. Why does she go to these countries? She wants to use her influence and visibility as a movie star to raise our awareness of other people's precarious situations.

> ANGELINA JOLIE TRAVELS THE WORLD TO AID POOR PEOPLE LIVING IN RURAL AREAS.

In 2006, Angelina created the Maddox Jolie-Pitt Foundation (MJP) to help with humanitarian crises around the world. The foundation gives money to organizations that help people affected by natural disasters or war. In 2007, MJP donated millions of dollars to SOS Children's Villages and the United Nations High Commissioner for Refugees to help displaced people in Darfur, and to Doctors without Borders in 2010 after the tragic earthquake that struck Haiti. ■

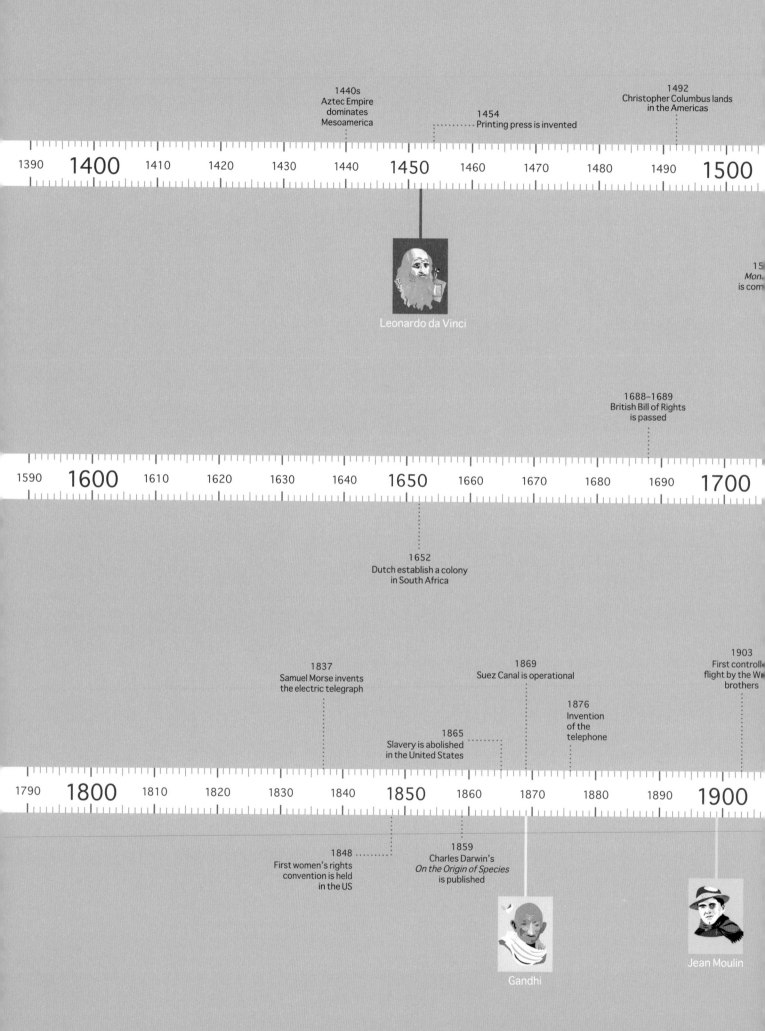

1440s
Aztec Empire
dominates
Mesoamerica

1454
Printing press is invented

1492
Christopher Columbus lands
in the Americas

1390 **1400** 1410 1420 1430 1440 **1450** 1460 1470 1480 1490 **1500**

15
Mon.
is com

Leonardo da Vinci

1688–1689
British Bill of Rights
is passed

1590 **1600** 1610 1620 1630 1640 **1650** 1660 1670 1680 1690 **1700**

1652
Dutch establish a colony
in South Africa

1837
Samuel Morse invents
the electric telegraph

1869
Suez Canal is operational

1903
First controll
flight by the W
brothers

1876
Invention
of the
telephone

1865
Slavery is abolished
in the United States

1790 **1800** 1810 1820 1830 1840 **1850** 1860 1870 1880 1890 **1900**

1848
First women's rights
convention is held
in the US

1859
Charles Darwin's
On the Origin of Species
is published

Gandhi

Jean Moulin

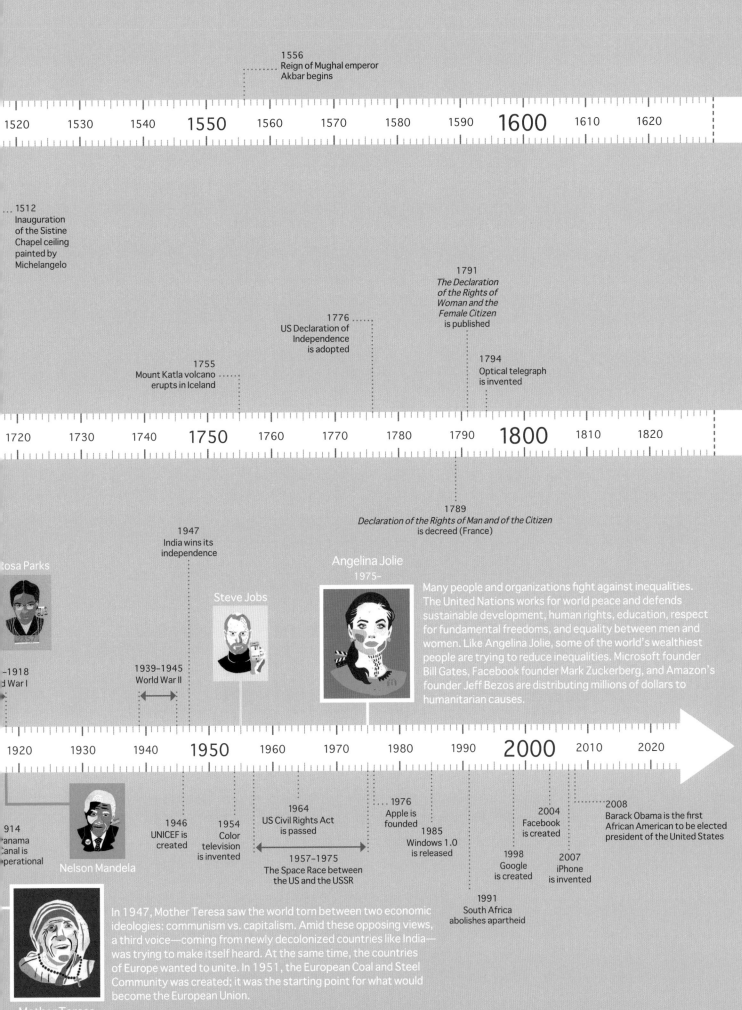

1556
Reign of Mughal emperor
Akbar begins

1520 1530 1540 **1550** 1560 1570 1580 1590 **1600** 1610 1620

… **1512**
Inauguration
of the Sistine
Chapel ceiling
painted by
Michelangelo

1791
*The Declaration
of the Rights of
Woman and the
Female Citizen*
is published

1776 ……
US Declaration of
Independence
is adopted

1794
Optical telegraph
is invented

1755
Mount Katla volcano ……
erupts in Iceland

1720 1730 1740 **1750** 1760 1770 1780 1790 **1800** 1810 1820

1789
Declaration of the Rights of Man and of the Citizen
is decreed (France)

1947
India wins its
independence

Rosa Parks

Angelina Jolie
1975–

Steve Jobs

Many people and organizations fight against inequalities.
The United Nations works for world peace and defends
sustainable development, human rights, education, respect
for fundamental freedoms, and equality between men and
women. Like Angelina Jolie, some of the world's wealthiest
people are trying to reduce inequalities. Microsoft founder
Bill Gates, Facebook founder Mark Zuckerberg, and Amazon's
founder Jeff Bezos are distributing millions of dollars to
humanitarian causes.

1939–1945
World War II

–1918
d War I

1920 1930 1940 **1950** 1960 1970 1980 1990 **2000** 2010 2020

… **1976**
Apple is
founded

2008
Barack Obama is the first
African American to be elected
president of the United States

1946
UNICEF is
created

1954
Color
television
is invented

1964
US Civil Rights Act
is passed

2004
Facebook
is created

914
anama
Canal is
perational

1985
Windows 1.0
is released

1957–1975
The Space Race between
the US and the USSR

1998
Google
is created

2007
iPhone
is invented

Nelson Mandela

1991
South Africa
abolishes apartheid

In 1947, Mother Teresa saw the world torn between two economic
ideologies: communism vs. capitalism. Amid these opposing views,
a third voice—coming from newly decolonized countries like India—
was trying to make itself heard. At the same time, the countries
of Europe wanted to unite. In 1951, the European Coal and Steel
Community was created; it was the starting point for what would
become the European Union.

Mother Teresa
1910–1997

THEY WAY OF

Johannes Gutenberg and Mark Zuckerberg have last names that end with the same syllable, but they have much more in common than that. Each revolutionized the way we communicate with one another and the world.

Before Johannes's invention of movable type, books were written by hand, and many people participated in their creation. First, a parchment maker prepared the writing materials from animal skins. Then, a copyist wrote the text, and an illuminator decorated the text with drawings. Finally, a binder attached the parchment sheets into book form. As you can see, writing a book in the Middle Ages was a long and slow process. To copy a Bible, for example, a monk had to work for about three years!

WITH NEW PRINTING TECHNOLOGY, NOW EVERYONE COULD OWN BOOKS.

The printing press was in use long before Johannes made his version. The process of copying texts by printing had already existed in Asia. In sixth-century China, people were reproducing images using woodblock printing, and in the eleventh century, banknotes were being printed.

So, why do we give so much credit to Johannes? The technology he developed helped automate and speed up the printing process. For example, he used a mixture of metals to create letters of type, which made them harder to damage during printing. As a result, it was possible to reproduce texts quickly and accurately.

Johannes
GUTENBERG

If you are holding this book, it is partly due to Johannes Gensfleisch zur Laden zum Gutenberg. Why so many words in his name, you may wonder. In the time and place where he lived, last names were not passed down from father to son. Instead, it was common to take the name of the family property. And that's how Johannes Gutenberg, the person who invented printing in Europe, got his long name.

Johannes was born around 1400 near the city of Mainz, Germany. We know little about his life, but we can imagine that he received a good education and probably even went to college. After a few years in Strasbourg, where he worked on his future inventions, Johannes returned to Mainz in 1448. There, he built his first printing press. To practice, he started by printing small texts, such as poems.

Johannes had borrowed money to build his press, and the time soon came for him to settle his debts. He needed to print a book that would make him money. The best-selling book in Europe at that time was the Bible.

On February 23, 1455, Johannes finished his first Bible. In all, he printed 180 copies, and forty-eight of those original books still exist today. But Johannes's project was not a success, and he could not repay his partner, who was furious. Johannes was sued, and his partner was awarded the printing shop by the court. Johannes then tried to launch another workshop in the town of Bamberg. Unfortunately, none of his printings were dated or signed, so it is difficult to identify the books and documents that came out of this workshop.

In 1465, Johannes was ennobled by the archbishop of Mainz and received a stipend. He had finally been recognized for his work! He died on February 3, 1468, and was buried in Mainz. His grave was lost when the church and cemetery were later destroyed.

Johannes GUTENBERG

(14th century–1468)

Mark ZUCKERBERG

+ ADD FRIEND

(1984–)

Mark ZUCKERBERG

You may not know Mark Elliot Zuckerberg personally, but you have certainly heard of his social network. With more than two billion members, Facebook is the most popular social network in the world.

First, let's go back in time. Mark was born on May 14, 1984, in White Plains, New York. As a boy, he was passionate about computers and even created software. He had inherited this love of technology from his father, who taught him programming.

In 2002, at age eighteen, Mark became a student at Harvard University. One evening, he downloaded ID photos of students living in the residence halls and posted them on the Web. He was nearly expelled for violating other people's privacy.

Cameron and Tyler Winklevoss, a pair of twin brothers, contacted Mark to ask for his programming help on a project. They wanted to develop a site called HarvardConnection that would link students with one another. Mark liked the idea so much that he decided to create his own platform.

And that is how thefacebook.com came to exist in 2004. Gradually, access was granted to more and more people: students from other universities and schools, companies such as Apple and Microsoft, and, finally, the general public in 2006. Facebook became a worldwide success.

(Did you know that Mark is colorblind, which means that he can't see certain colors well? The one he sees best is blue, which is why that color was chosen for the site.)

At only twenty-three years old, Mark became the youngest billionaire on the planet. In 2010, he was voted "Personality of the Year" and "Most Influential Person in the World" by *Time* magazine. In 2012, he married an American pediatrician of Chinese origin, Priscilla Chan, with whom he has two daughters. In 2015, Mark and his wife founded the Chan Zuckerberg Initiative. Its goal is to build a better future through equality, education, scientific research, health, and clean energy.

CHANGED OUR COMMUNICATING

In fifteenth-century Europe, the rewards of printing were immense. Now everyone could own books, and knowledge was no longer reserved for the elite members of society. A literate population did not need to depend on religious organizations such as the Catholic Church for education. About 20 million books were printed in Europe between the early days of printing and 1500.

FACEBOOK AND THE PRINTING PRESS CHANGED THE WAY WE COMMUNICATE.

Five hundred years later, Facebook was born. It was not the first social network to exist. Until 2004, Friendster was considered the number one social network; that was replaced by MySpace, Hi5, and Google Orkut. Some of these platforms disappeared, and Facebook beat out all the others. Today, the site is a giant—it's the third-most-visited website in the world (after Google and YouTube). Social networks like Facebook have changed the way we communicate. All age groups use the site to chat, play games, share videos, meet new people, or just talk about their lives without ever leaving home.

The widespread influence of Facebook can sometimes be problematic. For example, during the 2016 US presidential elections, Facebook was accused of manipulating public opinion by selling the personal data of millions of American users to outside companies. Those companies then displayed ads to influence the way people voted. We must all be careful what we share on social media and what we choose to "like."

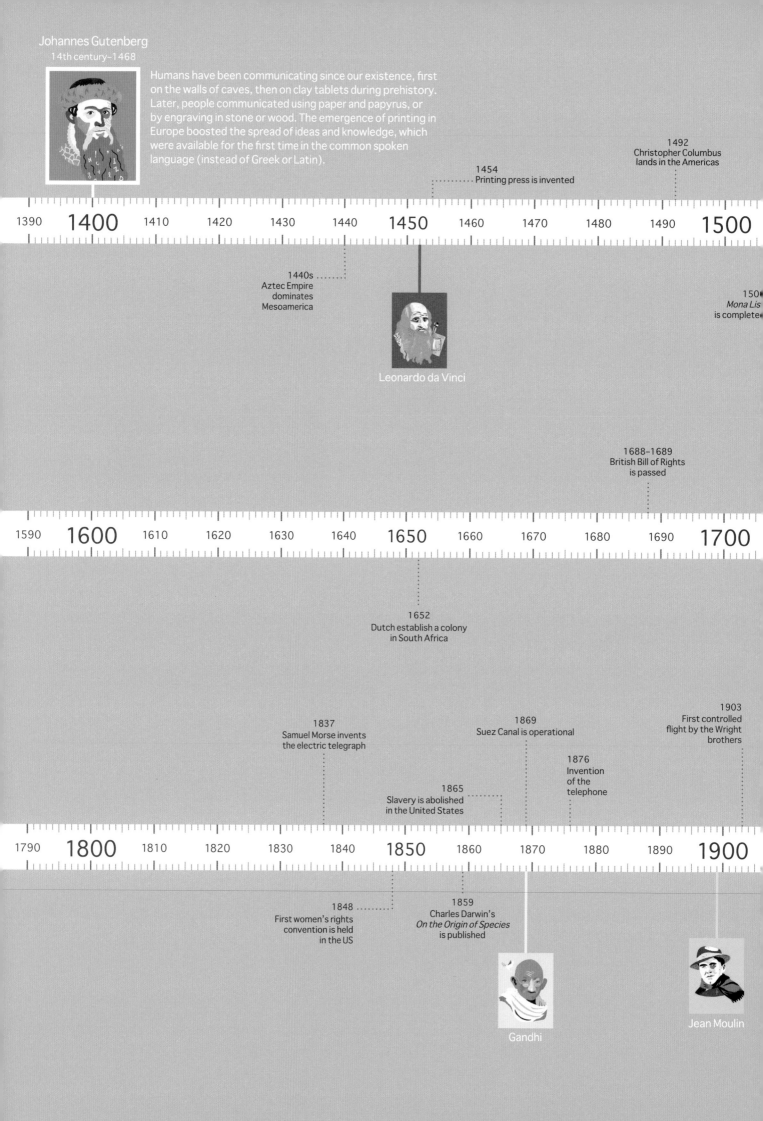

Johannes Gutenberg
14th century–1468

Humans have been communicating since our existence, first on the walls of caves, then on clay tablets during prehistory. Later, people communicated using paper and papyrus, or by engraving in stone or wood. The emergence of printing in Europe boosted the spread of ideas and knowledge, which were available for the first time in the common spoken language (instead of Greek or Latin).

1492
Christopher Columbus
lands in the Americas

1454
Printing press is invented

1390 1400 1410 1420 1430 1440 1450 1460 1470 1480 1490 1500

1440s
Aztec Empire
dominates
Mesoamerica

1500
Mona Lis
is complete

Leonardo da Vinci

1688–1689
British Bill of Rights
is passed

1590 1600 1610 1620 1630 1640 1650 1660 1670 1680 1690 1700

1652
Dutch establish a colony
in South Africa

1837
Samuel Morse invents
the electric telegraph

1869
Suez Canal is operational

1903
First controlled
flight by the Wright
brothers

1876
Invention
of the
telephone

1865
Slavery is abolished
in the United States

1790 1800 1810 1820 1830 1840 1850 1860 1870 1880 1890 1900

1848
First women's rights
convention is held
in the US

1859
Charles Darwin's
On the Origin of Species
is published

Gandhi

Jean Moulin

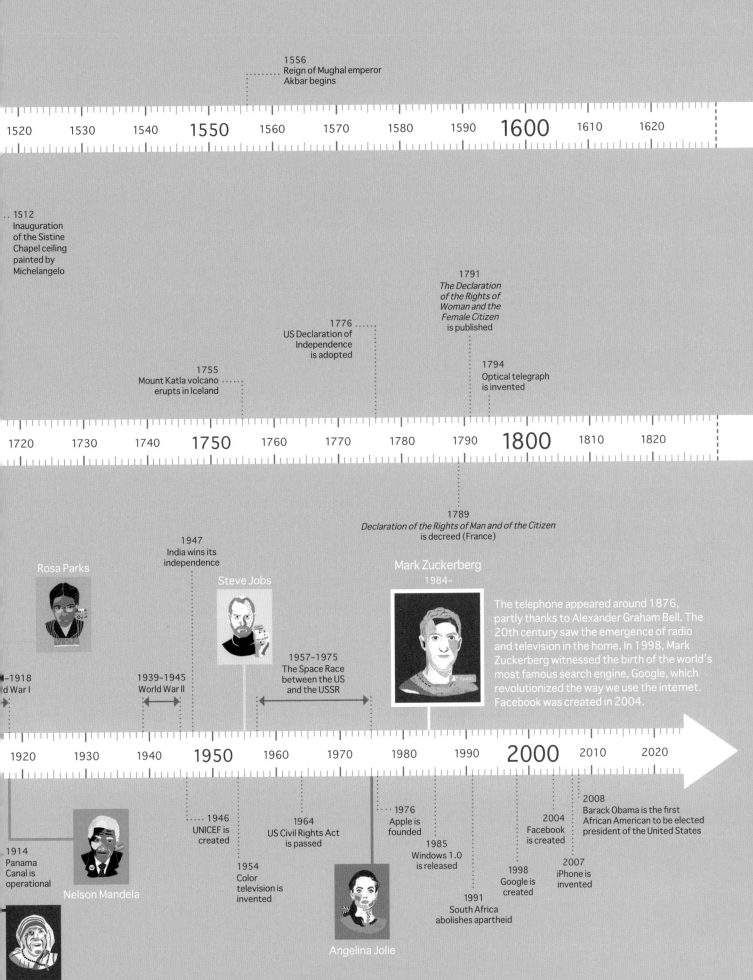

1556
Reign of Mughal emperor
Akbar begins

1520 1530 1540 **1550** 1560 1570 1580 1590 **1600** 1610 1620

1512
Inauguration
of the Sistine
Chapel ceiling
painted by
Michelangelo

1791
*The Declaration
of the Rights of
Woman and the
Female Citizen*
is published

1776
US Declaration of
Independence
is adopted

1755
Mount Katla volcano
erupts in Iceland

1794
Optical telegraph
is invented

1720 1730 1740 **1750** 1760 1770 1780 1790 **1800** 1810 1820

1789
Declaration of the Rights of Man and of the Citizen
is decreed (France)

Rosa Parks

1947
India wins its
independence

Steve Jobs

Mark Zuckerberg
1984–

The telephone appeared around 1876,
partly thanks to Alexander Graham Bell. The
20th century saw the emergence of radio
and television in the home. In 1998, Mark
Zuckerberg witnessed the birth of the world's
most famous search engine, Google, which
revolutionized the way we use the internet.
Facebook was created in 2004.

4–1918
d War I

1939–1945
World War II

1957–1975
The Space Race
between the US
and the USSR

1920 1930 1940 **1950** 1960 1970 1980 1990 **2000** 2010 2020

1946
UNICEF is
created

1964
US Civil Rights Act
is passed

1976
Apple is
founded

2008
Barack Obama is the first
African American to be elected
president of the United States

2004
Facebook
is created

1914
Panama
Canal is
operational

1954
Color
television is
invented

1985
Windows 1.0
is released

1998
Google is
created

2007
iPhone is
invented

Nelson Mandela

1991
South Africa
abolishes apartheid

Angelina Jolie

Mother Teresa

THEY WAY OF LOOKING

Charles Darwin and Galileo Galilei have one special thing in common: their fathers wanted them to become doctors. Unfortunately for their fathers, Galileo and Charles took a chance and decided their own destiny. The first turned his eyes to the stars, the second to Earth's fauna and flora. What were the consequences? Both challenged accepted ideas and revolutionized the way we see the world around us.

Charles Darwin was not the first person to talk about natural evolution. In the early 1800s, Jean-Baptiste Lamarck had described a theory of the evolution of living beings. But most people were not yet ready to accept his ideas. By the time Charles's theories were read in the 1860s, education in Europe had evolved. For many, faith in science was slowly replacing faith in the Christian Bible.

Charles understood natural selection after a long journey to the Galápagos Islands, in the Pacific Ocean. While there, he noticed that the beaks of finches had a different shape depending on which island they lived on. He concluded that the birds' geographical isolation and different diets led to the development of distinct species from the same ancestors. He found more than a dozen different finches. One type had a very thin beak that enabled it to feed on cacti and flowers. Another had a large beak for opening seeds. Still another kind had a sharp beak to better catch insects.

> CHARLES DARWIN AND GALILEO GALILEI OBSERVED THE WORLD CLOSELY AND CHANGED HOW WE SEE IT.

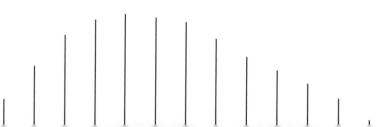

Galileo GALILEI

If you like stargazing, you may have already heard of Galileo Galilei. He was born in Pisa, Italy, on February 15, 1564. Galileo's father was a lute player, composer, singer, and music teacher. His parents taught him until he was ten years old, when the family moved to Florence. Galileo then received a religious education and began a career in the Catholic Church, which didn't last long. His father wanted him to become a doctor.

In 1581, Galileo began studying medicine at the University of Pisa, but he was not really interested in this field. He preferred math and was fascinated by astronomy and physics. Galileo's passion for these subjects caused him to rethink his studies. He returned to Florence in 1585 without a medical degree but with a growing mathematical knowledge.

From 1589 to 1592, Galileo taught at the University of Pisa, and he was a teacher at the University of Padua from 1592 to 1610. It was during this time that he made important discoveries. Galileo was one of the first people to use a telescope and turn it toward the sky.

When he did, he saw that the moon had many craters and that the Milky Way galaxy was made up of many stars that were invisible to the naked eye. In 1610, he discovered four satellites of Jupiter, which are the moons that we now call Io, Europa, Ganymede, and Callisto.

The more Galileo observed the sky, the more he realized that the sun was at the center of the universe, with the Earth and the planets orbiting around it. Impossible! The Roman Catholic Church and most scientists believed that the Earth was at the center of the universe; it was motionless, and the sun and other planets revolved around it. This idea is called geocentrism. Religious officials said that Galileo's heliocentric (sun-centered) view went against the Bible's teachings, a serious charge at the time.

In 1633, Galileo appeared before the Inquisition court to defend himself. He refused to deny his beliefs and was sentenced to house arrest in Tuscany. He was also forbidden to speak of his theories for the rest of his life. He died on January 8, 1642, at age seventy-seven.

Galileo GALILEI

(1564–1642)

Charles DARWIN

(1809–1882)

Charles
DARWIN

Do you have a collection? If you do, you'll probably never beat the one that Charles Robert Darwin amassed. After a five-year journey around the world, he brought home 3,907 specimens of animals and plants. He spent his life studying nature to understand how living things evolve, or change, over time.

Charles was born on February 12, 1809, into a wealthy family in England. He didn't like school; he preferred to collect beetles and minerals and to observe birds. His father was a doctor and wanted his son to follow his example. So, in 1825, Charles left to study medicine in Edinburgh, Scotland. He was not interested in his studies and wanted to learn taxidermy, the art of stuffing dead animals to give them the appearance of being alive. He helped with the research of zoologist Robert Edmond Grant, took courses in geology, and learned about plant classification.

Charles's father tired of his son's lack of progress and sent him to Cambridge to study theology. Once again, Charles preferred a different path. He took courses in botany and natural history, but he was still able to earn a diploma in theology in 1831. That same year, Charles decided to leave as a naturalist on board a Royal Navy ship for a voyage around the world. His job was to describe and inventory all the animals, plants, and rocks found during the five-year trip.

By the time he returned to England in October 1836, Charles was on his way to becoming a respected scientist. His observations had led him to form his theory of natural selection. This concept states that living beings that are best adapted to their environment will have the greatest chance to survive and reproduce. According to Charles, natural selection was the main driver of evolution. The idea that nature evolves was relatively new at the time, and it contradicted the teachings of the Catholic Church and some scientists, who believed that nature was fixed, as God created it.

In 1859, Charles published his theories in the book *On the Origin of Species*. He published more books on evolution and botany as well. He died on April 19, 1882, and is buried in Westminster Abbey in London. In the last years of his life, Charles saw most scientists accept his theories, which are now established as a foundation of modern science.

REVOLUTIONIZED OUR
AT THE WORLD

These discoveries proved, in Charles's view, the theory of evolution. Even if his ideas were criticized, more and more scientists accepted them as fact.

Galileo was less fortunate. His claims about heliocentrism (that the sun, and not the Earth, is at the center of the universe) were unacceptable in the 1600s. He was even convicted for publishing his theories. In January 1610, Galileo pointed his telescope at Jupiter and discovered its four moons. He was convinced that not all stars and planets revolved around the Earth. He said that Earth could not be motionless, and it was not at the center of the universe, which was being taught at the time.

Galileo was unable to prove his claims, which was why scientists and religious authorities did not want to believe him. Galileo thought he could prove his hypothesis through the phenomenon of tides, which he believed resulted from the Earth's own rotation and its orbit around the sun. But if that were true, there would be only one tide per day, not two. Galileo had forgotten to include the moon in his calculations.

Still, Galileo's contribution to science was important. His theories were later strengthened by Johannes Kepler, who discovered that the planets follow an elliptical path, and Isaac Newton, who founded the theory of gravity. Newton's theory explains why this book will fall to the ground if you drop it: because a body much bigger than it is—the Earth—attracts it. ■

Johannes Gutenberg

1454
Printing press is invented

1492
Christopher Columbus
lands in the Americas

1390 1400 1410 1420 1430 1440 1450 1460 1470 1480 1490 1500

1440s
Aztec Empire
dominates
Mesoamerica

Leonardo da Vinci

150(
Mona Li
is complete

1688–1689
British Bill of Rights
is passed

1652
Dutch establish a colony
in South Africa

1590 1600 1610 1620 1630 1640 1650 1660 1670 1680 1690 1700

Charles Darwin
1809–1882

Charles Darwin lived during the Industrial Revolution. Europe's population was growing rapidly, and progress was made in agriculture thanks to a new energy source—steam—that drove machines previously operated by people. It was the birth of industry, which also benefited transportation. Manufacturing, once carried out by hand, was now mechanized, leading to a new concept: mass production.

1903
First controlled
flight by the Wright
brothers

1869
Suez Canal
is operational

1876
Invention
of the
telephone

1865
Slavery is abolished
in the United States

1790 1800 1810 1820 1830 1840 1850 1860 1870 1880 1890 1900

1837
Samuel Morse invents
the electric telegraph

1859
Charles Darwin's
On the Origin of Species
is published

1848
First women's rights
convention is held
in the US

Gandhi

Jean Moulin

Galileo Galilei
1564–1642

In Galileo's time, witches were still being burned, the Earth was at the center of the universe, and medicine revealed human anatomy. Throughout Europe, a movement was spreading that challenged long-held scientific and philosophical ideas. This movement was accompanied by an artistic renewal that celebrated the art of ancient Rome and Greece: the Renaissance.

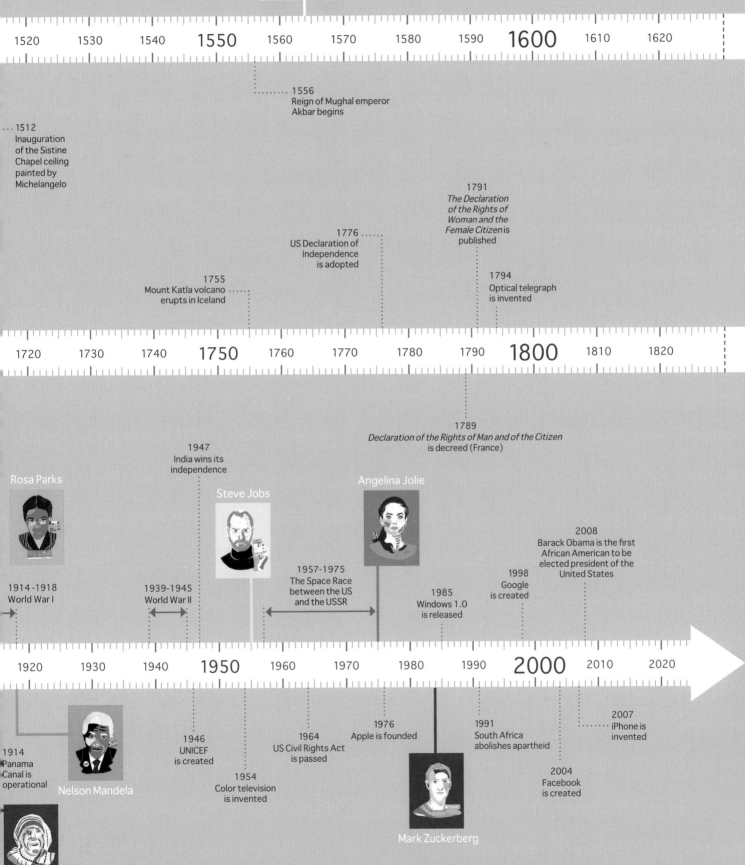

1520 1530 1540 **1550** 1560 1570 1580 1590 **1600** 1610 1620

1556
Reign of Mughal emperor
Akbar begins

1512
Inauguration
of the Sistine
Chapel ceiling
painted by
Michelangelo

1791
*The Declaration
of the Rights
of Woman and the
Female Citizen* is
published

1776
US Declaration of
Independence
is adopted

1755
Mount Katla volcano
erupts in Iceland

1794
Optical telegraph
is invented

1720 1730 1740 **1750** 1760 1770 1780 1790 **1800** 1810 1820

1789
Declaration of the Rights of Man and of the Citizen
is decreed (France)

1947
India wins its
independence

Rosa Parks

Steve Jobs

Angelina Jolie

2008
Barack Obama is the first
African American to be
elected president of the
United States

1957-1975
The Space Race
between the US
and the USSR

1998
Google
is created

1914-1918
World War I

1939-1945
World War II

1985
Windows 1.0
is released

1920 1930 1940 **1950** 1960 1970 1980 1990 **2000** 2010 2020

2007
iPhone is
invented

1946
UNICEF
is created

1964
US Civil Rights Act
is passed

1976
Apple is founded

1991
South Africa
abolishes apartheid

1914
Panama
Canal is
operational

1954
Color television
is invented

2004
Facebook
is created

Nelson Mandela

Mark Zuckerberg

Mother Teresa

THEY FOUGHT FOR

For several centuries, and even today, women and men have been fighting for equal rights. Olympe de Gouges is often thought of as one of the first feminists—people who fight for the improvement of women's roles and rights in society. The aim of feminism is to establish equality between men and women.

In addition to her fight for equality, Olympe fought for the right to divorce, the recognition of children born out of wedlock, and a system of protection for mothers. Today, in much of the world, even if this equality is not perfect, most of Olympe's wishes have been realized.

OLYMPE DE GOUGES IS CONSIDERED TO BE ONE OF THE FIRST FEMINISTS.

But in some places, deep inequalities still exist. That is why people like Emma Watson are committed to improving the status of women. Emma became interested in girls' education at a young age. She has visited Bangladesh and Zambia, and she uses her fame to attract the attention of the world to countries in need of help.

In September 2014, Emma delivered a keynote speech at United Nations headquarters in Washington, DC. In it, she called on men and women to make equality a priority. In the United States, women still do not enjoy the same rights and opportunities as men. There has never been a female

Olympe DE GOUGES

Olympe de Gouges was born Marie Gouze on May 7, 1748, in Montauban, in southwestern France. We know only a few details about her childhood. Her mother was Anne-Olympe Mouisset, but her father's identity is less certain. He could have been Pierre Gouze, who was a butcher or perhaps a lawyer. Olympe later claimed to be the illegitimate daughter of a local poet from the French nobility.

At age seventeen, Marie was forced to marry a much older man. He died a year later. At eighteen, she was already a mother and a widow.

Around age twenty, Marie met a man and moved with him to Paris, where she wanted to start a new life as a writer. She chose not to remarry. One reason was because French law did not allow a female author to publish her writings without her husband's consent. Marie also decided to call herself Olympe de Gouges, and she used this name to sign most of her writings and plays.

Olympe quickly set up her own theater company and began writing plays. Her first stage production was *Zamore and Mirza, or the Happy Shipwreck*, a play that denounced the enslavement of black people. Olympe made the play's title obscure to escape censorship. It was later revised to *Black Slavery, or the Happy Shipwreck*.

In 1789, the French Revolution broke out. Soon after, deputies of the new National Assembly wrote *the Declaration of the Rights of Man and of the Citizen*. Women were not mentioned in the text, which is why Olympe decided to write *The Declaration of the Rights of Woman and the Female Citizen*.

In 1793, the French Republic was less than a year old, and it was quite fragile. To protect it, authorities ordered the massacre of people still loyal to the monarchy. This violent period is called the Terror.

Olympe criticized the massacres and the Republic. As a result, she was arrested on July 20, 1793, and sentenced to death. She was guillotined on November 3, 1793, at the age of forty-five.

Olympe DE GOUGES

(1748–1793)

Emma WATSON

(1990–)

Emma WATSON

Wingardium leviosa! Let's talk about Emma Watson, who was born on April 15, 1990, in Paris. You know her from the role that made her famous: Hermione Granger, one of the three main characters in the eight Harry Potter films. Emma's parents are British lawyers who live in France. She has a brother, a half brother, and two half sisters.

At age five, Emma went to live in England with her mother when her parents separated. She attended a school with a magical name: the Dragon School. Unfortunately, there were no magic teachers—it was just a normal private school.

In 1999, during her school years, casting began for the film *Harry Potter and the Philosopher's Stone.* Emma passed eight auditions and was finally selected, out of 35,000 candidates, to play the role of Hermione. The movie was a huge success. Emma's school had to put rules in place to prevent the ten-year-old actress from being hounded for autographs by her classmates. Despite her success, Emma continued her studies, going on to graduate from Brown University in 2014.

By her twenty-eighth birthday, Emma had already starred in more than twenty movies, including *Beauty and the Beast* and *Little Women*. She has received many awards for her acting roles and has created her own clothing brand: Love from Emma.

In 2014, after visiting Bangladesh and Zambia to promote education for girls, Emma was named a Goodwill Ambassador for UN Women, a part of the United Nations. This organization fights for the inclusion of women in the economic and political life of their countries. It also contributes to improving the status of women and girls around the world.

Since September 20, 2014, Emma has been involved in a solidarity campaign that works for the equality of girls and boys. It is called HeForShe, and it aims to involve men in the fight for women's rights and equality between women and men.

WOMEN'S RIGHTS

president, and women still fight for equal pay, among other rights. In fact, a woman earns 20 percent less money than a man, on average, even if she has the same skills and does the same job. Equality between men and women is a long process that continues today.

In their everyday lives, many people around the world still believe in unfair ideas about men and women. For example, who says that girls should like fashion, dolls, romance novels, or horseback riding? Who says boys must like sports, trucks, bugs, or video games? Equality and freedom are about being able to choose whatever you want to do, be, wear, or like, according to your unique personality. ■

EMMA WATSON ADVOCATES FOR EVERYONE TO MAKE EQUALITY A PRIORITY.

EMMA WATSON AND OLYMPE DE GOUGES ARE KNOWN FOR THEIR WORK TO INCREASE EQUALITY AND OPPORTUNITIES FOR WOMEN.

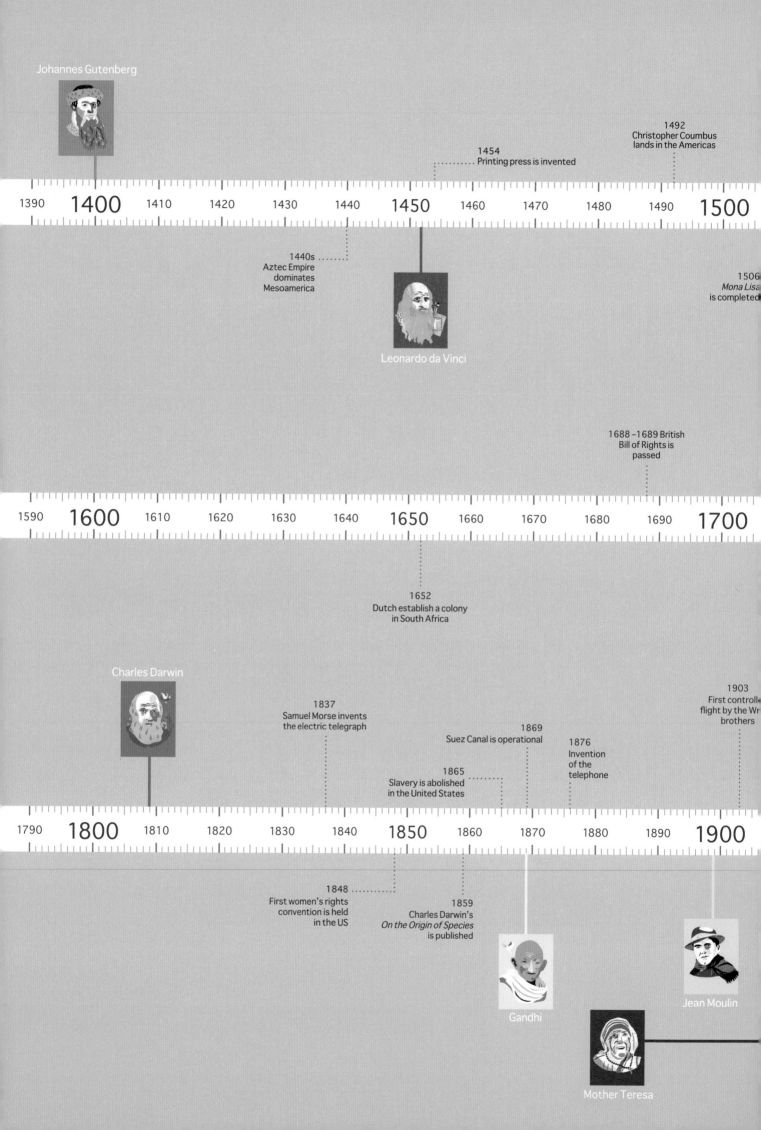

Johannes Gutenberg

1492
Christopher Coumbus
lands in the Americas

1454
Printing press is invented

| 1390 | 1400 | 1410 | 1420 | 1430 | 1440 | 1450 | 1460 | 1470 | 1480 | 1490 | 1500 |

1440s
Aztec Empire
dominates
Mesoamerica

1506
Mona Lisa
is completed

Leonardo da Vinci

1688 –1689 British
Bill of Rights is
passed

| 1590 | 1600 | 1610 | 1620 | 1630 | 1640 | 1650 | 1660 | 1670 | 1680 | 1690 | 1700 |

1652
Dutch establish a colony
in South Africa

Charles Darwin

1837
Samuel Morse invents
the electric telegraph

1869
Suez Canal is operational

1876
Invention
of the
telephone

1903
First controll
flight by the Wr
brothers

1865
Slavery is abolished
in the United States

| 1790 | 1800 | 1810 | 1820 | 1830 | 1840 | 1850 | 1860 | 1870 | 1880 | 1890 | 1900 |

1848
First women's rights
convention is held
in the US

1859
Charles Darwin's
On the Origin of Species
is published

Gandhi

Jean Moulin

Mother Teresa

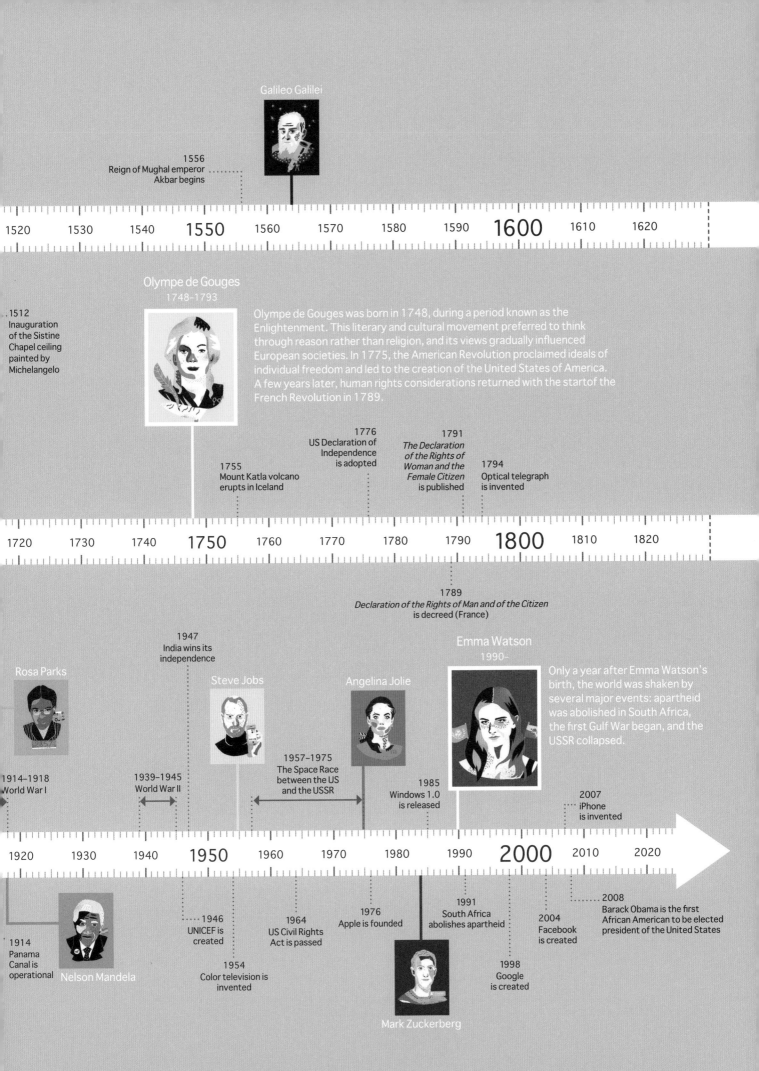

Galileo Galilei

1556
Reign of Mughal emperor
Akbar begins

1520 1530 1540 **1550** 1560 1570 1580 1590 **1600** 1610 1620

Olympe de Gouges
1748–1793

1512
Inauguration
of the Sistine
Chapel ceiling
painted by
Michelangelo

Olympe de Gouges was born in 1748, during a period known as the
Enlightenment. This literary and cultural movement preferred to think
through reason rather than religion, and its views gradually influenced
European societies. In 1775, the American Revolution proclaimed ideals of
individual freedom and led to the creation of the United States of America.
A few years later, human rights considerations returned with the start of the
French Revolution in 1789.

1776
US Declaration of
Independence
is adopted

1791
*The Declaration
of the Rights of
Woman and the
Female Citizen*
is published

1755
Mount Katla volcano
erupts in Iceland

1794
Optical telegraph
is invented

1720 1730 1740 **1750** 1760 1770 1780 1790 **1800** 1810 1820

1789
Declaration of the Rights of Man and of the Citizen
is decreed (France)

1947
India wins its
independence

Emma Watson
1990–

Rosa Parks

Steve Jobs

Angelina Jolie

Only a year after Emma Watson's
birth, the world was shaken by
several major events: apartheid
was abolished in South Africa,
the first Gulf War began, and the
USSR collapsed.

1914–1918
World War I

1939–1945
World War II

1957–1975
The Space Race
between the US
and the USSR

1985
Windows 1.0
is released

2007
iPhone
is invented

1920 1930 1940 **1950** 1960 1970 1980 1990 **2000** 2010 2020

1991
South Africa
abolishes apartheid

1976
Apple is founded

2008
Barack Obama is the first
African American to be elected
president of the United States

1946
UNICEF is
created

1964
US Civil Rights
Act is passed

2004
Facebook
is created

1914
Panama
Canal is
operational **Nelson Mandela**

1954
Color television is
invented

1998
Google
is created

Mark Zuckerberg

THEY SET

Do you get goosebumps reading about records being set and broken? You've come to the right place! Amelia Earhart and Felix Baumgartner set impressive records about a century apart.

Amelia began making history at the age of twenty-five, when she became the first woman to fly to an altitude of 14,000 feet. On May 20, 1932, she achieved another milestone. She took off from Newfoundland and Labrador, a Canadian province, for a nearly fifteen-hour flight to Northern Ireland. When she landed, she became the first woman to cross the Atlantic alone by plane. And that was just the beginning!

In January 1935, Amelia was the first person to successfully complete a solo flight from the island of Honolulu, Hawaii, to Oakland, California. It is a journey of roughly 2,000 miles across the ocean. Amelia participated in many long-distance races, taking these opportunities to beat speed and distance records.

> **AMELIA EARHART WAS THE FIRST WOMAN TO CROSS THE ATLANTIC ALONE BY PLANE.**

Amelia's most ambitious project was also her last: to fly around the world. The journey began on June 1, 1937. Amelia and her navigator flew across the United States, then down to Brazil and across the Atlantic to Africa. They flew over the Arabian Peninsula and crossed India and Oceania. Everything was going fine and the trip was almost over, but on July 2 the plane suddenly disappeared. Its signal was lost in the Pacific Ocean, where it was supposed to refuel on a small island

Amelia EARHART

If you want to break records someday, you can look to Amelia Mary Earhart as an example. She was born in Kansas on July 24, 1897. As a girl, she climbed trees, hunted rats, and cut out newspaper articles about women who succeeded in male-dominated professions, such as engineering, movies, and law.

In 1915, after Amelia had finished high school, the First World War was raging. She traveled to Toronto, Canada, and worked as a volunteer with wounded soldiers returning from Europe.

When she was twenty-three years old, Amelia got on a plane for the first time. That was the spark: she realized that she was born to fly! Amelia began taking flying lessons in January 1921. She worked several jobs and, within six months, had managed to buy her first plane. She decided to name it Canary because of its bright-yellow color. Amelia set her first record in this plane, reaching an altitude of 14,000 feet on October 22, 1922.

Charles Lindbergh made the first flight across the Atlantic Ocean in 1927, and Amelia wanted to be the first woman to do so. Five other women had tried before her, but none of them succeeded. Amelia started out in 1928, but the experience was frustrating. For safety reasons, she was accompanied by two male pilots, so she found herself a passenger in the plane, rather than the pilot.

In 1932, Amelia tried again, this time flying solo. She was the first woman, and only the second person, to succeed in a nonstop flight across the Atlantic. In the next few years, she set a series of records, proving that she could fly as well as any man.

In 1937, Amelia launched one final challenge: she wanted to be the first woman to fly around the world. It was during this journey that she disappeared on July 2, 1937. A rescue mission was sent out to find her, but the plane, its pilot, and her navigator were not located. Amelia's disappearance remains one of the great mysteries of our time.

Amelia EARHART

(1897–1937)

Felix BAUMGARTNER

(1969–)

Felix BAUMGARTNER

Perhaps you have seen the video of Felix Baumgartner's jump in free fall from the stratosphere, almost 128,000 feet above the Earth. It's so high that he had to wear an oxygen mask to breathe. This record jump made him famous.

Felix was born on April 20, 1969, in Salzburg, Austria. From a young age, he imagined himself flying. He made his first skydiving jump at sixteen years old, and since then he has been passionate about free fall.

After school, Felix worked as a mechanic and rode motocross before joining the Austrian army at the age of eighteen. During his military service, he became a paratrooper and took that opportunity to improve his skills. Jumping with a parachute is great, but he wanted more excitement. He started base jumping— jumping from a fixed site, like a tower or building, before deploying a parachute.

In 1996, Felix made his first base jump from the New River Gorge Bridge in the United States. It is the highest road bridge on the entire American continent and the second highest in the world, after the Millau Viaduct in France.

Felix became a professional base jumper in 1997 and set a series of records. It was not enough for him to jump from the second-highest bridge in the world, so he became the first person to jump from the Millau Viaduct in 2004. He entered into a partnership with a beverage company, which supported his project to break the record for the highest parachute jump. The jump was scheduled for 2012, and preparations with a team of scientists began in 2010. Two years later, Felix made test jumps, and then, on October 14, 2012, he made the jump from a helium balloon.

Felix made history that day, becoming the first person to break the sound barrier without a vehicle. Much scientific information was collected, too, that helps us understand how the human body is affected by extreme conditions. After completing his goal, Felix decided to stop extreme sports, though he still took part in difficult motor races, such as the twenty-four-hour Nürburgring. Today, he lives in Switzerland, where he devotes himself to some of his other passions: parachuting and helicopters.

RECORDS

before heading to Hawaii. For several days, dozens of planes and ships tried to find Amelia and her navigator, in vain.

Felix also set difficult goals. In 1999, at age thirty, he parachuted from the top of the Petronas Towers in Kuala Lumpur, Malaysia, setting the world record for the highest parachute jump. That same year, he set the world record for the lowest extreme jump by jumping from the hand of the *Christ the Redeemer* statue in Rio de Janeiro, Brazil. But if you think that's impressive, it's just the tip of the iceberg!

FELIX BAUMGARTEN WAS THE FIRST PERSON TO CROSS THE ENGLISH CHANNEL IN FREE FALL.

In 2003, Felix dropped from an aircraft at an altitude of more than 29,000 feet above Dover, England. He didn't open his parachute until about 3,000 feet, when he was above Calais, France. That made him the first person to cross the English Channel in free fall. He has also made extreme jumps: from the Millau Viaduct in France, the Turning Torso in Sweden, and the Taipei 101 tower in Taiwan, which was the world's highest building at that time.

Although today many of his records have been broken, including by Alan Eustace, who jumped from the stratosphere at a height of 134,000 feet, Felix remains a marvel in the world of extreme sports.

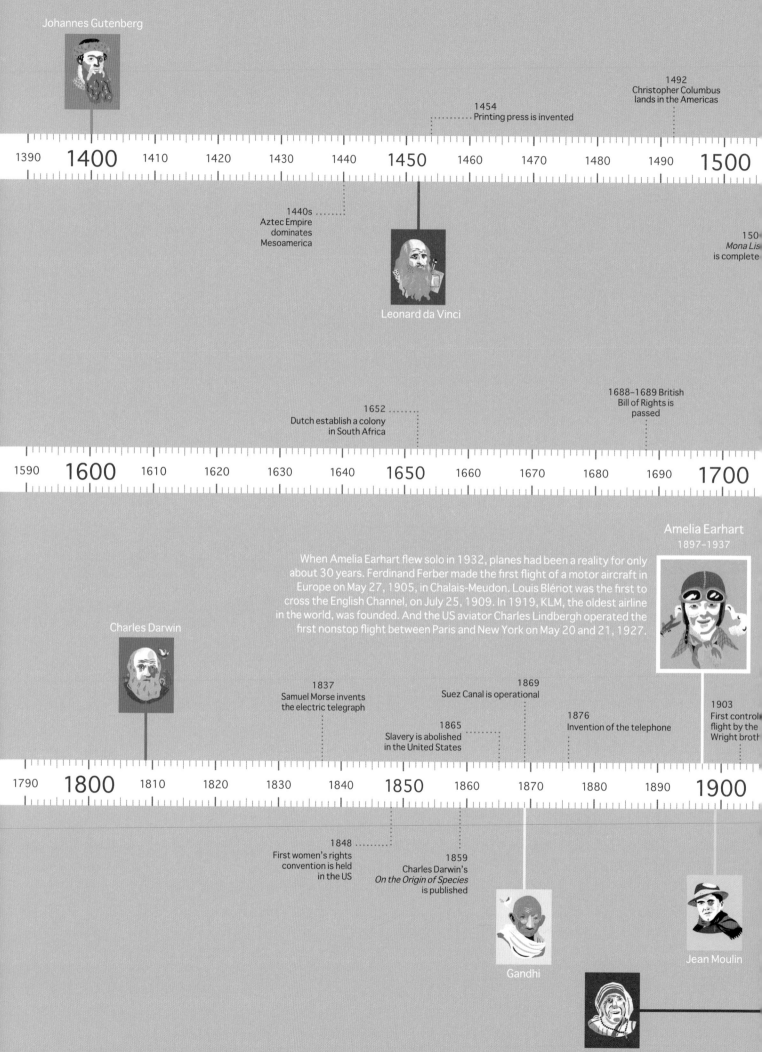

Johannes Gutenberg

1454
Printing press is invented

1492
Christopher Columbus
lands in the Americas

| 1390 | **1400** | 1410 | 1420 | 1430 | 1440 | **1450** | 1460 | 1470 | 1480 | 1490 | **1500** |

1440s
Aztec Empire
dominates
Mesoamerica

150
Mona Lisa
is complete

Leonard da Vinci

1652
Dutch establish a colony
in South Africa

1688–1689 British
Bill of Rights is
passed

| 1590 | **1600** | 1610 | 1620 | 1630 | 1640 | **1650** | 1660 | 1670 | 1680 | 1690 | **1700** |

Amelia Earhart
1897–1937

When Amelia Earhart flew solo in 1932, planes had been a reality for only about 30 years. Ferdinand Ferber made the first flight of a motor aircraft in Europe on May 27, 1905, in Chalais-Meudon. Louis Blériot was the first to cross the English Channel, on July 25, 1909. In 1919, KLM, the oldest airline in the world, was founded. And the US aviator Charles Lindbergh operated the first nonstop flight between Paris and New York on May 20 and 21, 1927.

Charles Darwin

1837
Samuel Morse invents
the electric telegraph

1869
Suez Canal is operational

1865
Slavery is abolished
in the United States

1876
Invention of the telephone

1903
First control
flight by the
Wright broth

| 1790 | **1800** | 1810 | 1820 | 1830 | 1840 | **1850** | 1860 | 1870 | 1880 | 1890 | **1900** |

1848
First women's rights
convention is held
in the US

1859
Charles Darwin's
On the Origin of Species
is published

Gandhi

Jean Moulin

Mother Teresa

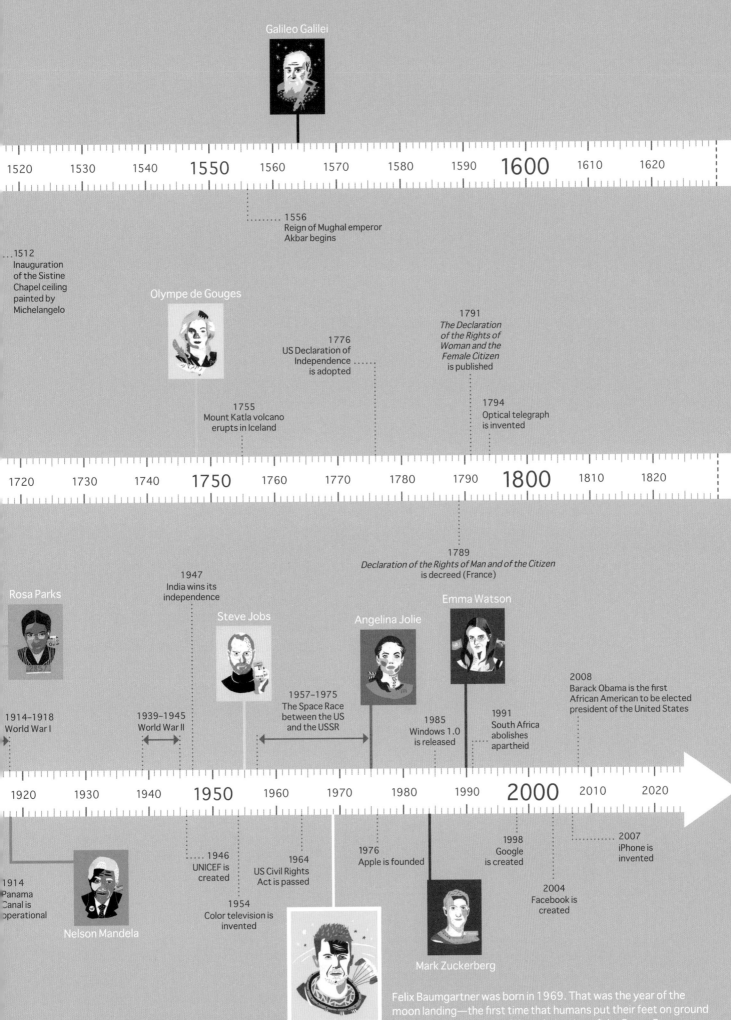

Galileo Galilei

1520 1530 1540 **1550** 1560 1570 1580 1590 **1600** 1610 1620

1556
Reign of Mughal emperor
Akbar begins

...1512
Inauguration
of the Sistine
Chapel ceiling
painted by
Michelangelo

Olympe de Gouges

1776
US Declaration of
Independence
is adopted

1791
*The Declaration
of the Rights of
Woman and the
Female Citizen*
is published

1755
Mount Katla volcano
erupts in Iceland

1794
Optical telegraph
is invented

1720 1730 1740 **1750** 1760 1770 1780 1790 **1800** 1810 1820

1789
Declaration of the Rights of Man and of the Citizen
is decreed (France)

Rosa Parks

1947
India wins its
independence

Steve Jobs

Angelina Jolie

Emma Watson

2008
Barack Obama is the first
African American to be elected
president of the United States

1914–1918
World War I

1939–1945
World War II

1957–1975
The Space Race
between the US
and the USSR

1985
Windows 1.0
is released

1991
South Africa
abolishes
apartheid

1920 1930 1940 **1950** 1960 1970 1980 1990 **2000** 2010 2020

1946
UNICEF is
created

1964
US Civil Rights
Act is passed

1976
Apple is founded

1998
Google
is created

2007
iPhone is
invented

1914
Panama
Canal is
operational

Nelson Mandela

1954
Color television is
invented

2004
Facebook is
created

Mark Zuckerberg

Felix Baumgartner
1969–

Felix Baumgartner was born in 1969. That was the year of the
moon landing—the first time that humans put their feet on ground
other than the Earth, and the culmination of the Space Race
between the US and USSR. Felix made his famous jump in 2012, the
same year that the rover *Curiosity* landed on Mars.

THEY RISKED
LIVES

Whereas Maurice and Katia Krafft preferred the heat of a volcano, the Earth's icy poles were the domain of Roald Amundsen. When talking about scientific advancements, all three are important.

If a volcano erupted somewhere in the world, the Kraffts rushed there to study it. This husband-and-wife team saw and documented more than 150 eruptions during their twenty-five-year career as volcanologists. They won awards and left behind a collection of more than 200,000 photos and hundreds of hours of films about volcanoes. They also published books to educate the public about this subject.

The research done by Maurice and Katia has saved lives. Their film about the risks of erupting volcanoes was shown to people in the Philippines not long before Mount Pinatubo erupted there in 1991. Partly thanks to this movie, the local authorities decided to evacuate nearby residents, and only 300 people were killed by the eruption. The explosion was so strong that the ashes released into the atmosphere lowered global temperatures by 1°F for three years. The mountain even lost 984 feet of its height!

THANKS TO THE KRAFFTS' FILMS, THOUSANDS OF PEOPLE HAVE ESCAPED HARM FROM EXPLODING VOLCANOES.

On June 3, 1991, on the slopes of Mount Unzen, in Japan, the Kraffts saw a phenomenon known as pyroclastic flow. They were unable to rent a helicopter, so they had to film from the ground. They didn't know it, but they were right in the path of destruction that would take their lives.

Maurice and Katia KRAFFT

Maurice and Katia Krafft were well-known volcanologists who devoted their lives to the study of volcanoes. Their work earned them the nickname Volcano Devils.

Both were born in the Alsace region of eastern France—Katia on April 17, 1942, and Maurice on March 25, 1946. Growing up, Maurice got interested in volcanoes on a family trip to Italy, where he witnessed the eruption of Mount Stromboli. As a teen, he joined the Geological Society of France and later studied geology in college.

Katia was passionate about volcanoes from a young age, too. When she was thirteen, she saw a dormant volcano for the first time in the Massif Central region of France. In 1960, during a trip to Italy, she visited Mount Etna and the ruins of Pompeii, a city that had been destroyed by a volcanic eruption during ancient times. This experience strengthened her choice to become a volcanologist. She later studied geochemistry at the University of Strasbourg.

Katia and Maurice met in 1966 through a mutual friend named Roland Haas. Two years later, calling themselves the Vulcan Team, the three friends organized excursions and scientific expeditions to erupting volcanoes. Their first trip was to Iceland, and in 1969 they took part in their first television show.

In 1970, Maurice and Katia married. Together, they studied and filmed more than 150 eruptions worldwide. They also wrote books and articles, made documentaries, and participated in TV broadcasts and conferences.

On June 3, 1991, tragedy struck. Maurice and Katia were trapped and killed by a pyroclastic flow on the slopes of Mount Unzen, in Japan. A pyroclastic flow is a mixture of volcanic gases, ash, and boulders that can reach a speed of 310 mph and a temperature of nearly 1,000°F. Maurice, Katia, and about forty other people had no chance to escape. But their research lives on and has greatly advanced our knowledge of volcanoes.

Maurice and Katia KRAFFT

(1946–1991)

(1942–1991)

Roald AMUNDSEN

(1872–1928)

Roald
AMUNDSEN

Do you like the cold and snow? Roald Engelbregt Gravning Amundsen did, too. He was born on July 16, 1872, near Oslo, Norway. As a boy, Roald dreamed of becoming a polar explorer, and he devoured books by John Franklin, an English explorer. He also admired the explorer Fridtjof Nansen, who returned triumphant from a 49-day ski trip across Greenland in 1889.

At sixteen, Roald wanted to experience a polar expedition. He and some classmates left for a hike through the mountains that lasted several days. His mother was critical of his interest in the polar regions. After he finished high school in 1890, she encouraged him to study medicine. Roald enrolled in college but left after three years for life as a sailor.

From 1897 to 1899, Roald took part in his first scientific expedition to Antarctica, sailing aboard the *Belgica*. The ship was caught in the ice pack, but the crew survived thanks to the doctor on board and by eating penguin meat. As soon as he arrived home, Roald prepared an expedition of his own. He wanted to find a maritime passage between the Atlantic and the Pacific via the Arctic Ocean.

Roald left in 1903 on his ship, the *Gjøa*, and was the first person to navigate the Northwest Passage, an exploit that was not repeated until 1977. When he returned home, he decided to tackle his life's dream: to be first to reach the North Pole. Unfortunately, as he was preparing his expedition, two other explorers beat him to it. In April 1909, Frederick Cook and Robert Peary both claimed to have reached the North Pole.

So, Roald decided he would be the first person to reach the South Pole. The expedition left on June 6, 1910, and landed in January 1911. The explorers installed a base camp to spend the polar winter. On October 20, 1911, Roald left for the pole, which he reached on December 14. But Roald wanted more challenges. So, he crossed the Northwest Passage in 1918, and attempted to fly over the North Pole in 1925 and again in 1926. He disappeared at sea in 1928, on his way to assist an Italian expedition that had flown over the Arctic.

THEIR FOR SCIENCE

Roald Amundsen died in the icy waters of the Arctic Circle. From each of his expeditions—the Belgian Antarctic Expedition (1897–1899), the Northwest Passage (1903–1906), and the South Pole (1910–1912)— Roald and his teams brought back valuable scientific data that improved our knowledge of the poles and polar ice caps. His greatest achievement was to reach the South Pole, but it was a close call. He learned that a British explorer named Robert Scott had the same goal. The race was on!

The two rival expeditions landed in Antarctica in January 1911, about 60 miles apart. Both set up a base camp to plan their route and spend the winter. Roald set off on October 20, with four companions and four sleds, each pulled by thirteen dogs. Robert Scott left on November 1, traveling with Siberian ponies. After more than 620 miles, Roald's expedition was the first to reach the South Pole, where they planted the Norwegian flag. The British team arrived on site one month later, but never returned home.

THE RESEARCH DONE BY ROALD AMUNDSEN
AND MAURICE AND KATIA KRAFFT HAS
CONTRIBUTED TO A GREATER UNDERSTANDING
OF THE NATURAL WORLD.

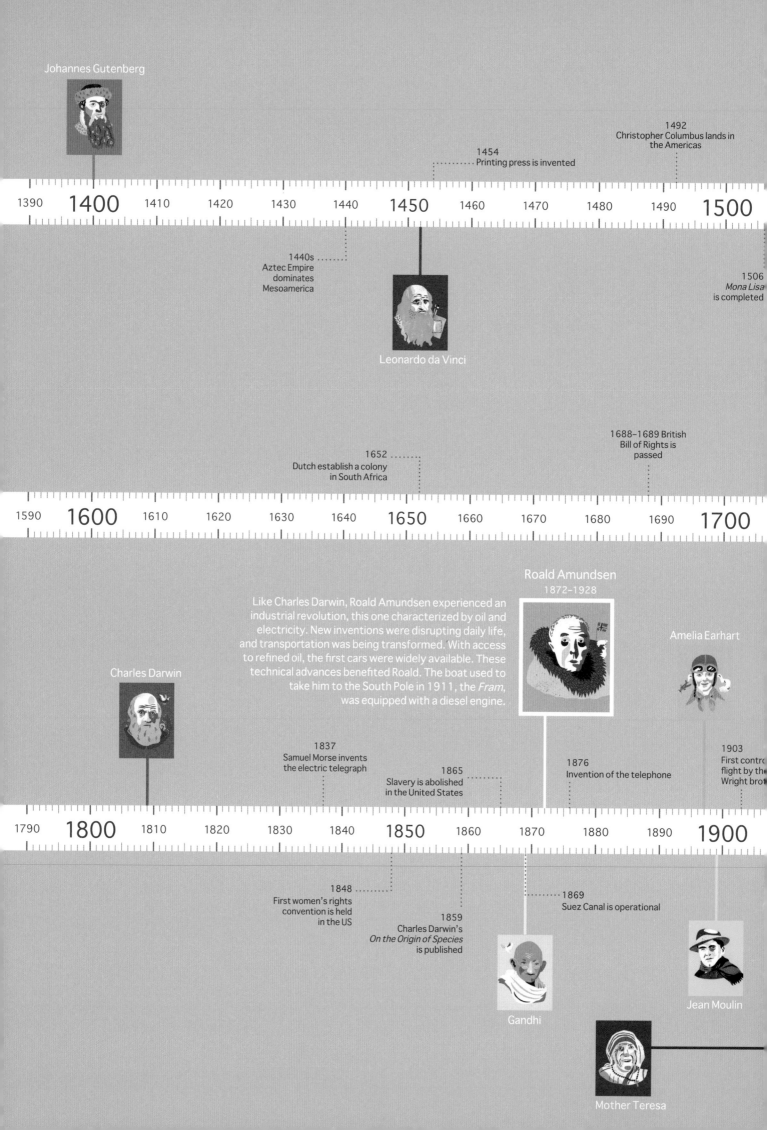

Johannes Gutenberg

1492
Christopher Columbus lands in
the Americas

1454
Printing press is invented

1390 **1400** 1410 1420 1430 1440 **1450** 1460 1470 1480 1490 **1500**

1440s
Aztec Empire
dominates
Mesoamerica

1506
Mona Lisa
is completed

Leonardo da Vinci

1688–1689 British
Bill of Rights is
passed

1652
Dutch establish a colony
in South Africa

1590 **1600** 1610 1620 1630 1640 **1650** 1660 1670 1680 1690 **1700**

Roald Amundsen
1872–1928

Like Charles Darwin, Roald Amundsen experienced an
industrial revolution, this one characterized by oil and
electricity. New inventions were disrupting daily life,
and transportation was being transformed. With access
to refined oil, the first cars were widely available. These
technical advances benefited Roald. The boat used to
take him to the South Pole in 1911, the *Fram*,
was equipped with a diesel engine.

Amelia Earhart

Charles Darwin

1837
Samuel Morse invents
the electric telegraph

1865
Slavery is abolished
in the United States

1876
Invention of the telephone

1903
First contro
flight by the
Wright bro

1790 **1800** 1810 1820 1830 1840 **1850** 1860 1870 1880 1890 **1900**

1848
First women's rights
convention is held
in the US

1859
Charles Darwin's
On the Origin of Species
is published

1869
Suez Canal is operational

Gandhi

Jean Moulin

Mother Teresa

Galileo Galilei

1556
Reign of Mughal emperor
Akbar begins

| 1520 | 1530 | 1540 | **1550** | 1560 | 1570 | 1580 | 1590 | **1600** | 1610 | 1620 |

.. 1512
Inauguration
of the Sistine
Chapel ceiling
painted by
Michelangelo

Olympe de Gouges

1791
*The Declaration
of the Rights
of Woman and the
Female Citizen*
is published

1776 .....
US Declaration of
Independence
is adopted

1755
Mount Katla volcano
erupts in Iceland

1794
Optical telegraph
is invented

| 1720 | 1730 | 1740 | **1750** | 1760 | 1770 | 1780 | 1790 | **1800** | 1810 | 1820 |

1789
Declaration of the Rights of Man and of the Citizen
is decreed (France)

1947
India wins its
independence

Rosa Parks

Steve Jobs

Angelina Jolie

Emma Watson

1957–1975
The Space Race
between the US
and the USSR

2008
Barack Obama is the first
African American to be elected
president of the United States

914–1918
World War I

1939–1945
World War II

1985
Windows 1.0
is released

| 1920 | 1930 | 1940 | **1950** | 1960 | 1970 | 1980 | 1990 | **2000** | 2010 | 2020 |

1954
Color television
is invented

1976
Apple is
founded

2007
iPhone is
invented

..1946
UNICEF
is created

1964
US Civil Rights
Act is passed

1991
South Africa
abolishes
apartheid

2004
Facebook
is created

914
anama
anal is
perational

Nelson Mandela

Felix Baumgartner

1998
Google
is created

Mark Zuckerberg

Katia Krafft
1942–1991
Maurice Krafft
1946–1991

When Katia and Maurice Kraft were growing up, many Western countries
were emerging from the destruction of World War II. The years between
1945 and 1975 saw great economic growth and cultural changes. The
Kraffts witnessed Neil Armstrong's first steps on the moon, Nelson Mandela's
struggle in South Africa, and Rosa Parks's resistance in the United States.

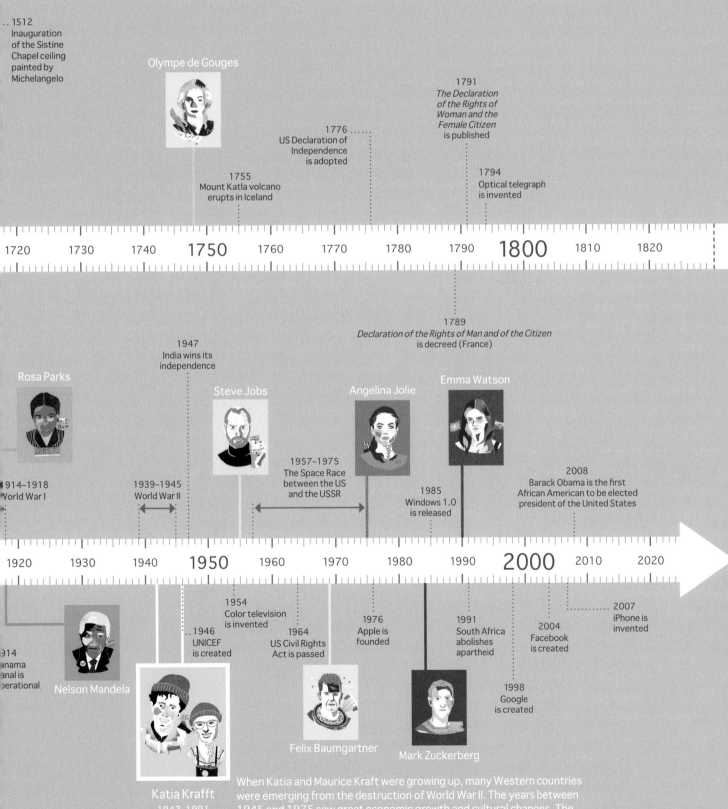

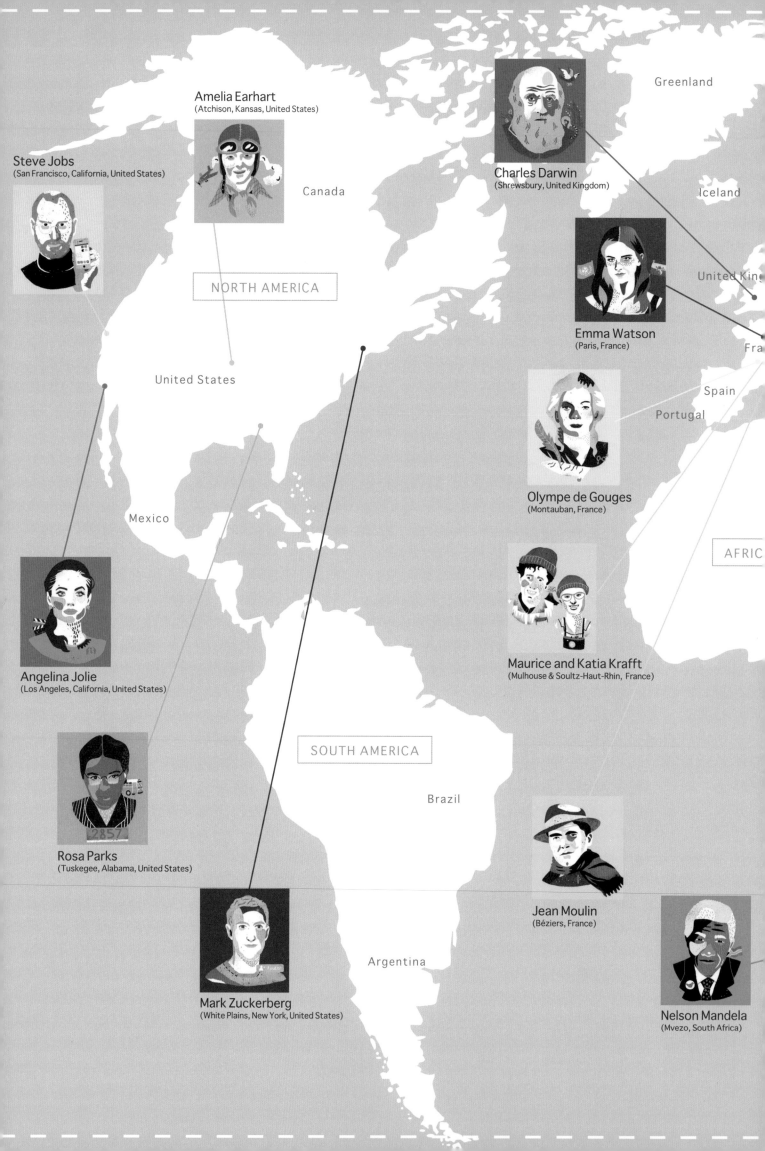

Amelia Earhart
(Atchison, Kansas, United States)

Steve Jobs
(San Francisco, California, United States)

Charles Darwin
(Shrewsbury, United Kingdom)

Greenland

Iceland

United Kin

Emma Watson
(Paris, France)

Fra

NORTH AMERICA

Canada

United States

Spain

Portugal

Olympe de Gouges
(Montauban, France)

AFRIC

Mexico

Maurice and Katia Krafft
(Mulhouse & Soultz-Haut-Rhin, France)

Angelina Jolie
(Los Angeles, California, United States)

SOUTH AMERICA

Brazil

Rosa Parks
(Tuskegee, Alabama, United States)

Jean Moulin
(Béziers, France)

Mark Zuckerberg
(White Plains, New York, United States)

Argentina

Nelson Mandela
(Mvezo, South Africa)

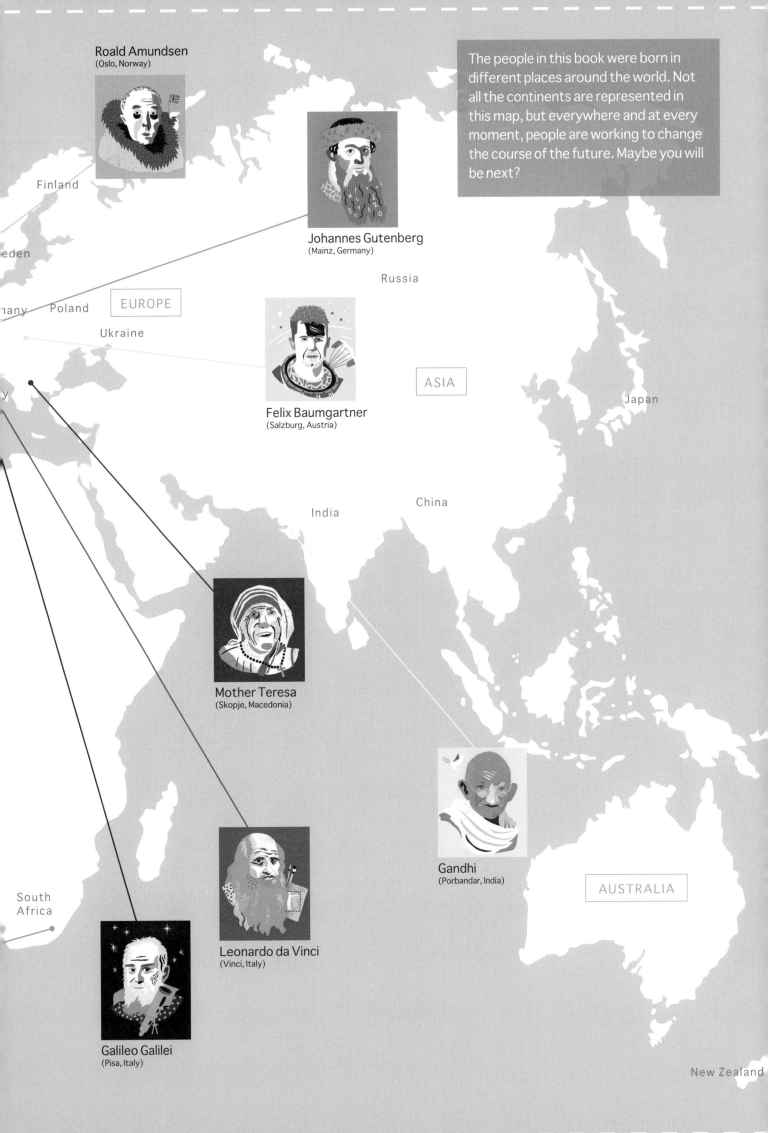

Roald Amundsen
(Oslo, Norway)

Johannes Gutenberg
(Mainz, Germany)

The people in this book were born in different places around the world. Not all the continents are represented in this map, but everywhere and at every moment, people are working to change the course of the future. Maybe you will be next?

Finland

Russia

eden

Germany   Poland   EUROPE

Ukraine

ASIA

Felix Baumgartner
(Salzburg, Austria)

Japan

China

India

Mother Teresa
(Skopje, Macedonia)

Gandhi
(Porbandar, India)

South Africa

Leonardo da Vinci
(Vinci, Italy)

AUSTRALIA

Galileo Galilei
(Pisa, Italy)

New Zealand

About the AUTHOR

Baptist Cornabas was born in Germany during the Cold War and became a European citizen at six years old. He earned a BA in literature, a BS in history, and an MS in teaching before beginning his career as a teacher. Two years later, he created his YouTube channel, *Parlons Y-Stoire*. This is his first book.

About the ILLUSTRATOR

Antoine Corbineau was born in 1982. A graduate of Camberwell College of Arts in London and the École supérieure des arts décoratifs in Strasbourg, he has worked with leading design and advertising agencies around the world. His colorful and complex illustrations have appeared in the *New York Times*, *The Guardian*, and *Vanity Fair*, as well as the campaigns of major brands like Dior, Hermès, and Yves Rocher. After living in Strasbourg, London, New York, and Paris, Antoine now lives and works in Nantes, France.